IF THE
FOUNDATIONS
BE
DESTROYED

IF THE FOUNDATIONS BE DESTROYED

JAMES T. DRAPER
FORREST E. WATSON

OLIVER
NELSON

A Division of Thomas Nelson Publishers
Nashville • Atlanta • Camden • New York

Published in Nashville, Tennessee, by Oliver-Nelson Books,
a division of Thomas Nelson, Inc., and distributed in Canada
by Lawson Falle, Ltd., Cambridge, Ontario.

Printed in the United States of America.

Library of Congress Cataloging in Publication Data
Draper, James T. and Watson, Forrest E.
     If the foundations be destroyed.

     Bibliography: p.
     Includes index.
     1. Christianity—United States.   2. Church and
state—United States.   3. United States—History—
Philosophy.   I. Watson, Forrest E., 1935-
II. Title.
BR515.D75 1984   277.3   84-1067
ISBN 0-8407-9525-4

We gratefully acknowledge the assistance of the following:
David Dawn—Researcher
R. J. Rushdoony—Adviser/Historian
Otto J. Scott—Adviser/Historian

We are also grateful for
the support and encouragement
of
Bob J. Perry

CONTENTS

	Preface	ix
ONE	America's True Heritage	1
TWO	Providential Failures in Colonization	15
THREE	The Time Is Ripe	25
FOUR	Puritan Law and Growing Secularism	47
FIVE	Religious Faith and the American War for Independence	73
SIX	The Christian Union Established	81
SEVEN	From Chaos to Centralization	107
EIGHT	Turning Toward a Socialist America	129
NINE	The Unfinished Story	153
TEN	Fundamentals for the Future	169

PREFACE

There is a prevailing myth that the government of the United States is designed to be separated from all religion, and that this separation was deliberate on the part of the Founding Fathers. This is not true. The Founding Fathers were opposed to a king and to an established church. They were not opposed to a chief executive or to the Christian religion.

Their positions were based upon their knowledge, as British subjects, of the dangers inherent in a combination of government and a particular denomination which—when together—constrict the liberties of the people.

The theory of a Church separate from the State was first launched by Christianity and is a basic Christian principle. The Founders, being aware that the greatest danger to religious liberties comes from the usurpations of the State, included the First Amendment as a means of protecting the Church from the State. Knowing that the State needed no protection from the Church, the same Founders created the system of military chaplains, biblical oaths of office, prayers at the opening sessions of Congress, and other recognitions of the Christian nature of the new republic. One remarkable feature of the new nation's government was that—alone in all the history of the world—its laws contained no disabilities against adherents of other religions.

In its early period, Protestantism represented the majority of American Christians. Therefore a multiplicity of denominations was present in the land from its inception. This is because there are a great variety of doctrinal strands within the non-Catholic branch of the Christian church. This variety, integral to Christian freedom, made it officially impossible to favor one denomination over another. Within this diversity, however, some denominations achieved both enormous numbers and considerable cultural power and political influence. And in recent times some of these main-line churches have sought to curb the traditional individualism of American Christianity. But the key to America's strength has been individual rebirth in Christ.

As waves of secularization swept across Europe, spawning new scientific and societal theories, the traditionally religious and specifically Christian nature of the American people began to shift toward its contemporary emphasis upon therapy and social science.

These are the modern versions of ancient pagan heresies based upon the idea that man can be his own God, and master of his own salvation. This had its origins in the premise of Satan as set forth in the original great humanist manifesto, Genesis 3:1-5 KJV:

> Now the serpent was more subtil than any beast of the field which the Lord God had made. And he said unto the woman, Yea, hath God said, Ye shall not eat of every tree of the garden?
>
> And the woman said unto the serpent, We may eat of the fruit of the trees of the garden:
>
> But of the fruit of the tree which is in the midst of the garden, God hath said, Ye shall not eat of it, neither shall you touch it, lest ye die.
>
> And the serpent said unto the woman, Ye shall not surely die:
>
> For God doth know that in the day ye eat thereof, then your eyes shall be opened, and ye shall be as gods, knowing good and evil.

Every man is to be his own god, knowing or determining what is good or evil, right or wrong, for himself.

America was settled by men knowledgeable in this Scripture and its significance. Captain Edward Johnson summoned Christians to emigrate to America and work for Christ's kingdom:

> Christ Jesus intending to manifest his Kingly Office toward his Churches more fully than ever yet the Sons of men saw...stirres up his servants as the Heralds of a King to make this proclamation for Voluntiers as followeth.
>
> Oh yes! All you the people of Christ that are here Oppressed, Imprisoned and scurrilously derided, gather yourselves together, your wifes and little ones, and answer to your several Names as you shall be shipped for his service, in the Westerne World, and more especially for planting the United Collonies of new England; Where you are to attend the service of

the King of Kings, upon the divulging of this Proclamation by his Herralds at Armes....

Could Casar so suddenly fetch over fresh forces from Europe to Asia, Pumpy to foyle? How much more shall Christ who createth all power, call over this 900 league Ocean at his pleasure, such instruments as he thinks meete to make use of in this place....Know this is the place where the Lord will create a new Heaven, and a new Earth, in new Churches, and a new Common-wealth together.*

America was to be a center from which the whole world was to be brought under the lordship of Jesus Christ. The role of Americans in Christian missions has been a mighty one.

But there were problems. The Christian colonists wanted to order all of life, and their civil government, schools, churches, and communities, in terms of the Word of God. The Crown in England was consistently against this: the word of the king should have priority. There was thus a long struggle to maintain the freedom of the Word of God as the ruling word.

But this was not all. The hard work of the colonists almost at once led to prosperity, and many came who were more interested in getting rich than in serving the Lord. These men chafed at the "restraints" of a godly, moral order.

Another problem developed in the colonial period. The first settlers still thought in old European patterns. They were often against the Established Church in England or elsewhere, only because they wanted a different established church. They believed, as men had for generations, that Christianity flourished best if it were established from the top down. Believers arose to insist that the faith had to be established first in the hearts and lives of men. From that base there could be a remaking of churches, schools, and civil governments through their changed lives, reformation from the believer upward. A great champion of this cause, long neglected, was the Baptist leader Isaac Backus.

One result of all this was the First Amendment to the United States Constitution. It was included at the insistence of the clergy. It was intended to keep the federal government out of the life of the churches. Religious freedom was to be freedom from the State and its controls. In

---

*Albert Bushnell Hart, *American History Told by Contemporaries* (New York: Macmillan, 1897), vol. 1, pp. 366ff.

this century, this meaning has been reversed. The courts seem to view the First Amendment as no restraint upon the states and the federal government in their interference with the freedom of the faith. The First Amendment is seen as a restraint upon religion!

The early republic has been called "the happy republic." It was a free Christian country. The churches of the young United States early became zealous in missions. The role of American churches in world missions is one of the greatest in the history of Christianity. Christians led also in a wide variety of reforms, and the home missions and revivals were instruments whereby millions of immigrants as well as native unbelievers were converted to Christ. Year in and year out, the United States was flooded with immigrants, so that our population increased dramatically. Just as dramatically, these immigrants were brought to Christ in great throngs.

At the same time, humanism was also at work. The churches were committed to establishing a Christian realm from the ground up, by converting the people. The humanists, beginning with the Unitarian movement, were committed to salvation by law—statist law. Their faith was in the salvation of man by works of civil law from the top down. Toward this end, the humanists worked to gain control of civil government in order to save America according to their humanistic gospel. They also began to influence many churches.

The imprint of Christian faith, however, was on all America and her institutions. Thus, the task of the humanists has been a considerable one. Since World War II, they have been hard at work to dismantle Christian America and to create a Humanist America. In late 1983, Michael Harrington, a prominent leader in Washington politics, wrote a book called *The Politics at God's Funeral*. God is dead, says Harrington, and we had better bury Him. Long-accepted social and moral values, laws with biblical origins, and much more are still influencing western civilization. These must be rooted out. There must be a united front of all men to create a new society based on the death of God. This new society will deny God-given law and morality in favor of allowing men to discover their own values. There will be no absolute truth, only situational and personal determination of truth.

Here again we have the original humanist manifesto: "...ye shall be as gods [or God], knowing good and evil" (Genesis 3:5 KJV).

To be a Christian in America is to be on a great battlefield. This book is about the history of that battlefield, the great achievements which have made America strong and godly, and the evils now threatening her life. To be effective in that holy warfare, we must understand what it is about, and what was accomplished by our Christian forefathers. We must also see what remains for us to do in this conflict. This is history written in an older Christian sense, for Christian soldiers engaged in serving their Lord and King, who alone provides salvation for men and nations. This is not a book for armchair readers who will read and then shelve it. It is for Christians who believe that "whatsoever is born of God overcometh the world, even our faith" (1 John 5:4).

As we go through the history of exploration, colonial history, the early republic, the conflicts of the last century, the world wars and their aftermath, our focus will be on the Christian influence in the past and our calling under God for the future.

In the Lord put I my trust: how say ye to my soul, Flee as a bird to your mountain?

For, lo, the wicked bend their bow, they make ready their arrow upon the string, that they may privily shoot at the upright in heart.

If the foundations be destroyed, what can the righteous do?

The Lord is in his holy temple, the Lord's throne is in heaven: his eyes behold, his eyelids try, the children of men.

The Lord trieth the righteous: but the wicked and him that loveth violence his soul hateth.

Upon the wicked he shall rain snares, fire and brimstone, and an horrible tempest: this shall be the portion of their cup.

For the righteous Lord loveth righteousness; his countenance doth behold the upright.

Psalm 11 KJV

America's True Heritage

Recent generations of Americans have, in general, either not known or not been taught the facts regarding the Christian influence in America's history. This has produced generations of persons ignorant regarding the providential founding of this great nation. Americans today are largely unaware of God's influence in the events which resulted in the creation of the United States of America.[1]

Beginning in the early nineteenth century, a deliberate effort was made to edit our Christian heritage out of textbooks. By 1860, Americans yielded to secular arguments and churches lost their leadership in education. Education became a governmentally dominated sector. This closed the Bible as the primary textbook in the land. Instead of building individual character based upon biblical principles, a shift was fostered toward building characters conformable to society. Thus, we shifted from a God-centered republic to a man-centered democracy. Seeds were planted to weaken the basic character of America.[2]

The Founding Fathers had a clear understanding of the concept of Christian character as the foundation of education. Today we have lost that foundation. National and state laws in America are such that our government schools, which teach approximately 85 percent of the nation's children, are forbidden by the courts to teach the principles upon which America was founded. Dr. Mark Fakkema points out the consequences of this development in his Introduction to *Teaching and Learning America's Christian History*. He says, "We as a nation have lost our former national conscience. It was for the purpose of preserving this conscience that our Founding Fathers came to this country."[3]

It is now more necessary than ever to restore the educational connec-

1

tion between Christianity, individual freedom, local self-government, and a strong republic. The failure to retain this connection, due to the secularization of all our societal institutions, is the basic reason the American people are unknowingly moving into socialism degree by degree.

In an excerpt from *The Christian History of the United States* Dr. Jedidiah Morse describes just such a time in an election sermon delivered in Charleston, April 25, 1799. Though the causes which had brought the people to this condition were quite different, the effect was very similar. Dr. Morse's Bible text was Psalms 11:3 KJV: "If the foundations be destroyed, what can the righteous do?" The following was included in his sermon:

> Our dangers are of two kinds, those which affect our religion, and those which affect our government. They are, however, so closely allied that they cannot, with propriety, be separated. The foundations which support the interest of Christianity, are also necessary to support a free and equal government like our own. In all the countries where there is little or no religion, or a very gross and corrupt one, as in Mohametan and Pagan countries, there you will find, with scarcely a single exception, gross ignorance and wickedness, and deplorable wretchedness among the people.
>
> To the kindly influence of Christianity we owe that degree of civil freedom and political and social happiness which mankind now enjoys. In proportion as the genuine effects of Christianity are diminished in any nation, either through unbelief, or the corruption of its doctrines, or the neglect of its institutions, in the same proportion will the people of that nation recede from the blessings of genuine freedom, and approximate the miseries of complete despotism. I hold this to be a truth confirmed by experience. If so, it follows, that all efforts made to destroy the foundations of our holy religion, ultimately tend to the subversion also of our political freedom and happiness. Whenever the pillars of Christianity shall be overthrown, our present republican forms of government, and all the blessings which flow from them must fall with them.[4]

Documented history since 1799 verifies Dr. Morse's observations. America's true history must be placed in the hands of the ordinary citizen such as John Wycliffe, who made the Bible available in 1382.

Prior to the Wycliffe Bible, kings and the clergy interpreted God's Word to the ordinary citizen. None but the elite had direct access to the Scriptures. The message in and through the Bible was left to an elite to know, and to pass on to those others they chose. The situation then was not too unlike America today regarding our Christian heritage.

Secular historians credit greed as the primary motive for the Age of Exploration. However, documents of the exploration period reveal that a desire to spread the Gospel of Christ was one of the stronger motivations that drove men to risk ventures into the unknown. This was primarily due to the access these men had to God's Word. It caused them to remember their Christian heritage and the principles upon which that heritage was based. That knowledge gave them purpose and direction. They knew the sacrifices that had been made for their salvation and spiritual freedom and were committed to extending the same to their fellowmen.

The new ideas thus started in the domain of religion soon communicated themselves to other spheres of men's lives. There then rose, above the existing tyrannical political world of the day, a class of thinkers who grasped the idea that the State ought to exist for man, that justice, protection, and the common good ought to be the aim of government.[5]

Perhaps if the true history of America's heritage is restored to the ordinary man, a reformation will occur today that will return the country to biblical principles.

The Myths of Spanish America

The fact is that secularistic histories have given us a falsified picture of both Spanish and Catholic America as well as of Protestant and English America. The caricatures of the Spanish colonies and of the Puritan settlers are often not only incorrect but malicious as well.

For example, the Puritans in England and America are presented as sour killjoys. The fact is that in their day the Puritans were regarded as the friends of the workingman because of their insistence on the Sabbath rest *and* days of recreation. As Percy A. Scholes pointed out in *The Puritans and Music in England and New England* (1934), the Puritans in 1647 made by law a requirement that every second Tuesday of the month was to be a day's holiday for students, apprentices, servants, and all. If some "extraordinary occasion" made work necessary on that day, another day had to be set aside for recreation and play. This is hardly a publicized fact about Puritans, and this is but one of a multitude of omissions!

Let us begin with the truth about Spanish America. One area of American history about which there are many myths made and believed concerns the Spanish explorers and colonists. The Spanish discovery, exploration, and colonization of America are badly misrepresented in books, schools, and the media. While the Spanish were not perfect, they were far more humane and Christian than the "Black Legend" would have us believe. Let us survey the Spanish period by dealing with some of these myths.

The Flat World Myth

"The world is flat," so men then held, according to a popular myth. European men before Columbus did not know what lay beyond the shores of the Atlantic, but they did not believe the earth was flat.

Columbus was a constant reader, particularly of books dealing with geography and related subjects. These works all taught that the earth was round. For example, Pythagoras, in the sixth century B.C., taught that the world was round. Aristotle came to his belief in a sphere-shaped planet by observing the shape of the shadow the earth made on the moon during a lunar eclipse. Plato, Virgil, and Ovid are three more ancient writers who understood the shape of the world.[6]

Another real influence on the minds of men was the Bible. While the Bible is not a geography book, there are casual references to the subject within its pages. Because the men of Columbus's day believed that God wrote the Bible through His apostles and prophets, they knew that everything it said must be true. Isaiah 40:22 NKJV is a verse which shows the greatness of God by citing the wonders of His creation. It says, "It is He [God] who sits above the circle of the earth, And its inhabitants are like grasshoppers, Who stretches out the heavens like a curtain, And spreads them out like a tent to dwell in." The Hebrew word translated "circle" is *kuwg*, meaning a sphere. This verse is not saying that God sits above a world which is shaped like a circle drawn on a piece of paper. It describes God as being above a world shaped like a ball.[7]

There were popular geography books in Columbus's day which also insisted on a spherical earth. Ptolemy's *Geography*, although written in the second century A.D., was widely read in the 1400s and held that the world was a perfect sphere. Europe and Asia, wrote Ptolemy, were one continuous land mass running west to east. He also taught that between Western Europe and the east coast of Asia there was an ocean. This view was also held by Pierre d'Ailly, author of *Description of the World*. In this book, evidence is brought forward from observations made by Greeks and Arabians confirming the roundness of the earth. His theories were not exactly right, however. He held that the distance between Spain and India was not great and could be sailed in a few days.[8] Views of the earth's size, *not* its shape, were in error.

There was another book Columbus was familiar with, one which hit even closer to the truth. It was called *Universal History*, written by Aneas Sylvius Piccolomini (later to become Pope Pius II). This book discussed the possibility of a "new" continent, as yet undiscovered. This raises an interesting point. Did Columbus ever realize that the discovery he made of the New World was not part of Asia or the Pacific Islands? The answer is emphatically yes. When Columbus, on his second voyage, landed on the American mainland at the mouth of the Orinoco River in Venezuela, he knew he was on a continent. He wrote in his diary for August 14, 1498, "I believe that this is a very large continent which until now has remained unknown." Columbus had a better grasp of the situation than we are sometimes led to believe.[9]

The flat-earth idea is a myth which denigrates medieval men. This, however, is not the only myth about Columbus and the other Spanish explorers. The other myths are more serious, having to do with questions of a moral nature.

The Gold Myth

It has been taught that the Spanish were interested in the New World because they wanted gold and would do anything for it. They would kill or enslave Indians, commit any outrage, simply to get gold. Motives for exploration are not always easily discerned. "Because it's there" is a popular way of explaining man's desire to go where no man has gone before. Another motive certainly was economic. The Spanish and other explorers wanted raw materials to export back to Europe.

They also wanted gold and silver for their treasuries. Another important economic motive was the desire to find a shorter route to the Far East.

There was, however, another motive, one not often discussed. Almost to a man, with the exception of Francisco Pizarro, those early Spanish explorers were concerned over missionary work. They wanted to spread the Christian Gospel to those remote people who had never heard of Jesus Christ. Columbus certainly was anxious to become involved in this good work.[10] Part of the reason Ferdinand Magellan, the explorer whose ships were the first to sail around the world, lost his life was his interest in preaching the Gospel to the natives.[11]

When Nicolas de Ovando was sent by Queen Isabella in 1502 to be governor of Hispaniola (Dominican Republic and Haiti), she made her purposes clear. Her "principal intention" in sending this governor was the conversion of the natives.[12] How one wishes that even a tiny fraction of America's diplomatic activity today had such a high goal!

The Ruthless Killer Myth

The Ruthless Killer Myth is a very serious charge. This myth charges that the Spanish came to America and at once started to kill all the Indians. The Indians are said to have been innocent, uncorrupted people leading peaceful and happy lives. The Spanish came and destroyed their way of life forever. We are told that not only were many killed but the Spanish also infected these poor natives with all the sinful vices of the Europeans. Let us examine what some call one of the worst episodes of all: the Spanish conquest of Mexico. Some writers give the impression that Hernán Cortés, leader of the conquest, would have felt at home in Stalin's KGB. What are the facts?[13]

At the time Cortés arrived in Mexico, the land was ruled by the Aztec Indians. Far from having had a one-thousand-year-old empire, the Aztecs had only overpowered Mexico with their army about a century before the Spanish arrived.[14] Also, there was little love for the Aztecs among most of the Indian tribes in the land. At various times Cortés had up to seventy-five thousand Indians with him as allies against the Aztecs. One can hardly say the Spanish ruthlessly destroyed an ancient and peaceful empire.

None of the Aztecs or their Indian enemies were all that civilized or friendly; they were at first all quite hostile to the Spanish. The general pattern of Cortés's relations with a tribe went something like this: Cortés would make an offer of friendship, which was refused. The Indians, desiring captives for human sacrifice or cannibal feasts, would then attack the Spanish. Cortés and his men, numbering no more than five hundred, would have to defend themselves. Time after time, they managed to win battles with great loss of life to the Indians. The Indian tribes would send thousands of warriors against the small Spanish band, but after the battle, the Indians and the Spanish would work together for peace. The natives would lavish great hospitality on their former enemies and, in return, Cortés would teach them about the Christian faith. Not only would he encourage them to give up their idols and the practice of human sacrifice but he would also work to make them a part of a new country.

After many such efforts, the Spanish reached Tenochtitlán, now better known as Mexico City, a beautiful city which greatly impressed Cortés and his men. Mexico City was built on an island in a lake, reached by various causeways from the shore. The buildings were monumental, and the whole city was clean. Montezuma, the chief of the Aztecs, received the Spanish with great ceremony. Not only did he provide food for them but he also allowed them to live in a huge palace once used by his father.

Through interpreters, Cortés talked to Montezuma about the Christian faith. They discussed such doctrines as the Trinity, the creation of the world, and the birth, death, resurrection, and ascension of our Lord Jesus Christ for the sins of mankind. Cortés also urged Montezuma to stop worshiping idols and to put an end to human sacrifice and cannibalism. Montezuma hedged at this point, although it is said that he gave up eating a favorite dish of his, made with the meat of young boys.

After some time, the Spanish began to suspect that they, too, were being fattened up for some sacrifice or feast. This feeling was probably encouraged by sights such as human hearts smoking in urns at the temples. Another disturbing incident was a report by friendly Indian messengers from the coast where Cortés had left a small garrison of troops. They were told that Quauhpopca, one of Montezuma's chiefs, had attacked this post, killing a Spanish captain.

Cortés took immediate action. Being as polite as possible, he put Montezuma and his harem under "house arrest" and moved them to the palace where the Spanish were living. After the first shock, Montezuma seemed to have accepted the situation. He continued to provide food for his captors and maintained good relations with Cortés. He even agreed with Cortés's demand that Quauhpopca and his accomplices be executed.

At this point, Cortés himself left for the coast to deal with another troop of Spanish soldiers sent to Mexico by a suspicious Spanish governor. Upon his return to Mexico City, he found the place in uproar. In his absence, the officer in charge had prevented the Aztecs from holding one of their religious festivals which involved human sacrifice. The whole city, all three hundred thousand people, rioted. To fight this vast mob was impossible, so Cortés asked for a truce. His request was refused. Cortés then had Montezuma speak to his people, but his subjects now felt this chief was a traitor because of his friendship with the Spanish; they attacked him with spears and rocks. He died of his wounds three days later. There was nothing more to be done. With great loss of life, Cortés and his men fought their way out of the city and fled to a friendly Indian village to recover.

Subsequently Cortés, his small band of men, and seventy-five thousand Indian allies returned to Mexico City. Cortés tried every peaceful way he could to get the city to surrender, but it refused. The Spanish then laid siege to the city. They did, however, leave one causeway open so that any who wished to could escape the Spanish. The Aztecs did not avail themselves of this escape route.

It was a long, bloody siege, with great loss of life. The cries of Spanish soldiers who had been captured could be heard from outside the city. These captives were sacrificed in a most sadistic manner, and some were eaten. The tortured screams from the city must have had an effect on the soldiers which we can only imagine. The Aztecs began tossing the remains of these captives over the walls at the besieging army.

Small wonder that, when Mexico City finally fell, there was a slaughter of fifteen thousand Aztecs. Cortés had told his troops not to take revenge, but there was no holding back his Indian allies. However, when Cuauhtemoc, son of Montezuma, was recaptured leaving the city, Cortés treated him with all the respect due the leader of a great nation.

The Spanish then set about rebuilding the city, placing Christian churches where once there had stood heathen temples. Far from following a "burnt earth" policy, Cortés was anxious to help the Indians

8

rebuild their shattered homes. He was also concerned with teaching them the Christian religion. It is true that there was a period when Indians were mistreated; Cortés was out of the country from 1524 to 1530, leaving men with less kindness in command. But the practice followed by the explorers and those who set Spanish policy was one of charity, help, and Christian missionary work.

This story destroys several myths. First of all, we look at the Spanish expedition. In a difficult situation, the Spanish worked to keep loss of life to a minimum. Their behavior stands in stark contrast to the common picture painted of them as bloodthirsty killers. On the other hand, we see that the popular idea of an ancient empire living in peace and plenty is false. The Aztec empire was young and dominated its subjects by military force. The other Indians flocked to aid Cortés by the thousands. We see that the myth of the "noble savage"—innocent and virtually without sin until the Europeans came—is false. The Indians, as we have pointed out repeatedly, were guilty of many crimes against their own people. It was the Spanish who tried to stop these cannibalistic practices and teach them the Christian way of life. We have been given myths as history.

The Slavery Myth

When the average person thinks back to the days of Spanish America, the image which comes to mind is often one of harsh taskmasters abusing their Indian slaves. This myth, often called the "Black Legend," comes down to us through the writings of an earnest Catholic priest named Bartolomé de Las Casas. Las Casas, who spent most of his adult life in America, had a growing horror of slavery, which made him highly sensitive to every injustice committed by his nation. He was equally blind to the many good things which Spain did. From his pen, tales of wrongdoing told with emotions running high have come down through centuries to a secure place in the public mind.

Before discussing the slavery issue, let us examine a few historical details.[15] We have already mentioned Queen Isabella's instructions to Governor Nicolas de Ovando when she sent him to govern Hispaniola. Along with her instructions regarding the conversion of the Indians to Christianity, she also gave directions about putting the Indians to work. She pointed out that the Indians on Hispaniola were lazy and would not work, even for wages. As a result they avoided contact with the Spanish altogether. This obviously made their conversion to Christianity impossible. Therefore, she commanded that the Indians be made to live with the Christians and work for them in their farms and mines. However, they were to be considered free people and not slaves. This was the beginning of what was called the "encomienda system," regarded by Las Casas as a great evil.

Things took a turn for the worse for the Indians when Queen Isabella died in 1504. At that time her husband, Ferdinand, whose main interest was gold, became regent of the Indies. Under Ferdinand, Indians were treated badly. They were forced to work in the mines until they died. A steady stream of slaves was brought in to maintain the number of miners. At one point, to have enough workers, whole tribes were brought in from the Bahamas as slaves.

The Spanish, a proud people, refused to work in the fields to grow food because too many saw themselves as gentlemen. Because the Indians were too "lazy" to toil for them, even for wages, the Spanish used harsh methods to force the Indians to tend the crops.

There is, however, another side to this story. The Spanish government was ready to listen to complaints about the way Indians were treated. They were also prepared to act. In 1512, a Dominican friar named Antonio de Montesinos came to Spain and preached about what he felt were the terrible conditions of the Indians in Hispaniola. Ferdinand was very moved by his account. After consulting with theologians and scholars, he proclaimed a new code of laws dealing with the Indians. These statutes were called the Laws of Burgos, after the town in which Ferdinand proclaimed them. They were intended to provide protection for the Indians. These laws did not end encomiendas or slavery, but they did limit the number of slaves per person to 150.

In 1515, Montesinos again went to Spain, accompanied this time by Las Casas. Las Casas had an audience with Ferdinand on Christmas Eve. He told the regent that the encomiendas were destroying the Indians and that the Laws of Burgos were not working to defend them. Ferdinand was impressed by Las Casas and promised to meet him again after Christmas. But Ferdinand died on January 25, 1516, before he saw Las Casas. One thing these two incidents show is the openness of even someone like Ferdinand to the problems of the Indians.

In 1542, Las Casas had another victory. This time he persuaded King Charles V of the need for reform. So it was that on November 20,

1542, at Barcelona, the king proclaimed the New Laws. These regulations prohibited any more slaves from being taken, even from among prisoners of war. In addition, efforts would be made to investigate the ownership of existing slaves with a view to their liberation. Indians could not be forced to be burden bearers, except in emergencies. Also, because of high Indian death rates, natives of Hispaniola, Puerto Rico, and Cuba would be exempt from taxes. These laws provoked rebellions in Peru and Mexico. Neither these protests nor the risk of losing its empire stopped the Spanish government from its mission of helping the Indians.[16]

Las Casas was not pleased. Fanatic reformers are often unreasonable, and Las Casas even managed to enrage his fellow missionaries. The famed Fray Toribio de Benavente, ministering in Mexico, wrote to the king, "I am astonished that Your Majesty and those of your councils have been able to suffer for so long a man in religious garb so offensive, restless, importunate, turbulent, pettifogging, disturbing, so bad mannered, abusive, injurious, and so lacking in tranquility."[17] When Las Casas was appointed bishop of Chippa, in the south of Mexico, he forbade the sacraments to be given to slaveholders. When the Dean of the Cathedral granted absolution to some of these men, Las Casas had him arrested. This led to a riot and the removal of Las Casas from the area. His zeal often hurt his earnest cause.

In the late sixteenth century, the Spanish put an end to a rebellion by the Chichimeca Indians of Mexico by kindness. After a long war that was impossible to win, the Spanish gave up fighting and tried giving gifts of food and clothing instead, with great success. The army became so popular with the Indians that it made sure there was a priest present at each gift-giving. This was in order to get the Indians to love the missionaries as they did the army! In gratitude, on one occasion, an Indian chief tried to give the army several children to cook and eat as a treat! This gives only an inkling of Chichimeca life, but it is the Spanish who are seen as inhumane.[18]

The facts about Indian slavery are important to understand. The Spanish really were concerned that the natives should become Christians. They felt that conquest was a means to that end. It insured that the Indians would live under a Christian government. The same was true of slavery. It wasn't only free labor which interested the Spanish. They felt that having the Indians live and work with them would be a good influence. The owners of slaves were obliged by law to teach their charges about Christianity and the Gospel. This was their sincere belief and practice. However wrong we may believe them to have been, we must recognize that the system was not as evil as some cases would indicate.

It must be borne in mind also that Indians were slaveholders, too. This was not a practice imported by the Spanish. In fact, many of the slaves had been bought by the Spanish from the Indians.

To end on a positive note, let us glance at two benefits which the Spanish brought to the New World. In the area of health care, historian Philip Wayne Powell quotes a Mexican university professor of pharmacology, "Lima, Peru, in colonial days had more hospitals than churches and averaged one hospital bed for every one hundred and one people, a considerably better average than Los Angeles [California] has today."[19] In education, the Spanish established twenty-three colleges and universities in the New World during the colonial era which graduated one hundred fifty thousand students. No other colonial power has such a record.[20]

In summary, remember, first, the most important motive behind Spanish exploration—despite its many failings—was the preaching of the Gospel to the heathen. Second, colonization was on the whole beneficial to the Indians; the Spanish treated them better than the Indians treated one another. The Spanish colonies were imbued with the premises of the Roman Catholic faith.

Some historians have held that Spain was far more fair in its treatment of the Indians than were the English colonies and, later, the United States. Without going into the merits of that argument, we can say this: the Spanish colonies had a more controlled policy. The Spanish crown governed Indian affairs conscientiously and carefully.

This usually was also true of the English Crown and, much of the time, the United States Congress when independence came. There was, however, a problem in the colonies and in what became the United States. Great masses of migrants pushed westward, disregarding the instructions of Crown and Congress. In addition, lawless men sought escape into the frontier. These men held that the rules of remote governors and authorities were irrelevant to their situation, and the results were often conflicts.

This points up a characteristic aspect of the American venture: its semblance at times of anarchy, but its fact of freedom. Where men act in freedom, they will create either havoc or a superior order, depending on their lack of faith or their zeal in Christian faith. Freedom has both perils and blessings. As opposed to State and Church as the power centers, Christianity in what became the United States developed instead a different priority, the conversion of individuals to Jesus Christ. The individual believer is to be the power center, the living temple of the Holy Spirit and a member of Jesus Christ who is King of kings and Lord of lords (Revelation 19:16). In such a society, greater good and greater evil are possible. Its presupposition is that, while the Lord works through all things in creation, persons are His primary instruments. This faith is the American story.

In a very real sense, Spanish America is a part of Europe. Its culture reflects the European patterns of Church and State, and its roots go deep into Europe's past. By comparison to Spanish America, the United States is a raw, young country. The American power and vitality come from a new step in the history of Christianity, one of faith working from the bottom up. In politics, it means an emphasis on localism, on city and county governments. In the Church, the stress is on the local church. In the manifestation of social energy and power, the heart of this faith is apparent: the power center is the man in Christ exercising his calling to bring all things in his life and world under the authority of Jesus Christ.

Chapter 1 Notes

1. Verna M. Hall, *Teaching and Learning America's Christian History* (San Francisco: Foundation for American Christian Education, 1965), p. XIII.
2. Ibid., p. XIX.
3. Ibid., p. XX.
4. Verna M. Hall, *The Christian History of the Constitution of the United States of America* (San Francisco: Foundation for American Christian Education, 1966), pp. IV, V.
5. Ibid., p. 2.
6. Samuel Eliot Morison, *The European Discovery of America—The Northern Voyages* (New York: Oxford University Press, 1971), p. 6.
7. Ibid., p. 6.

8. Felipe Fernandez-Armesto, *Columbus* (New York: Saturday Review Press, 1974), pp. 32–33, 37–38.
9. Ibid., pp. 40, 168.
10. Louis B. Wright, *Gold, Glory, and the Gospel* (New York: Atheneum Publishers, 1970), p. 62.
11. Ibid., pp. 158–159.
12. Ibid., pp. 208–209.
13. Ibid., chapter 9: "Hernán Cortés, Greatest of the Conquistadors," pp. 160–204.
14. Nigel Davies, *Voyagers to the New World* (New York: William Morrow, 1979), pp. 57, 96–97.
15. Wright, *Gold, Glory, and the Gospel*, chapter 10: "Bartolomé de Las Casas and the 'Black Legend,' " pp. 205–226.
16. Philip Wayne Powell, *Tree of Hate* (New York: Basic Books, 1971), p. 33.
17. Ibid., p. 35.
18. Philip Wayne Powell, *Mexico's Miguel Caldera* (Tuscon: University of Arizona Press, 1977), pp. 104, 146.
19. Powell, *Tree of Hate*, pp. 24–25.
20. Ibid., p. 25.

Providential Failures in Colonization

TWO

A serious mistake very often made is to judge the past by the present. If we use Boston today to judge the Puritan settlement of Boston, or Harvard today to govern our view of that college when the Puritans first established it, we will surely go astray. This is also true if we try to judge the early Spanish, French, and English explorers and settlers in terms of contemporary Latin America, Quebec, and the United States. As Spurgeon, quoting John Bunyan, reminds us, "Every tub must stand on its own bottom."

Why did the Age of Exploration begin only after 1492? Long before that time, Europe had discovered America; the Vikings, if not others, had landed here. Scholarly Europe was aware of some lands to the west, but until Columbus, no efforts were again made to explore the western seas and realms. Then suddenly everyone was interested.

The usual explanation was "gold fever." However, men began the western quest and exploration before any substantial gold was encountered in Mexico. The search for gold was very real, but why had it not impelled men one hundred or three hundred years earlier?

Let us remember that Columbus was moved to his task by the prophecies of Isaiah. He took with him Luis de Torres, who spoke Hebrew, in case they ran into some "lost tribes" of Israel. Not only Columbus but every Spanish explorer except Pizarro had missionary goals. When we read Hakluyt's many volumes of Voyages, we find the explorers of the various countries speaking often of Scripture and its prophecies. The modern scholar usually skips over these things to concentrate on economic motives, but no honest reading of the accounts of and about the explorers can escape the strongly Christian motive. Europe was in the

15

midst of a revival; people other than the clergy were concerned about the faith. Lay groups like the Brethren of the Common Life were growing. The explorers, for all their faults, shared in this missionary concern. The Reformation a generation after Columbus was one result; the Age of Exploration was another.

A neglected fact about the explorers of America is that many of them were deeply religious men. We have already seen this in our look at the Spanish, and the same is true of the men sent out by the French and the English. We are not talking about superstitious sailors but of true Christians committed to their faith and their God. Morison was quite right when he observed, "...every discoverer expected to play apostle to the Indians, and to find quantities of gold."[1] The truth about the explorers is that both aspects were important to them.

A look at two early French explorers will give us a couple of examples of the Christian faith at work in these voyagers. Giovanni da Verrazano, an explorer for France, in 1524 sailed the east coast of America from North Carolina to Maine, looking for a passage into the Pacific. Failing in that task, he discovered a vast new land, as yet only inhabited by Indians. Upon his return to France, he encouraged the king to further explore the discoveries made, quoting Romans 10:18.[2] This verse reads in the NKJV, "Their sound has gone out to all the earth, And their words to the ends of the world." Clearly, Verrazano had a knowledge of the Bible. There is no reason to doubt that he knew the meaning of this verse—the spreading of the Word of God through the entire world.

Ten years later, another French explorer, Jacques Cartier, showed a clear interest in missionary work among the natives. Upon making contact with the Micmac Indians on the shore of Chaleur Bay (on the north coast of New Brunswick Province), Cartier observed that the Indians were ready for conversion. A few days later he landed on the shore of Gaspe Harbour. There Cartier and his men raised a cross thirty feet high and knelt around it holding hands. With the Huron Indians looking on, the sailors motioned toward heaven, to show from where their salvation came.[3] This was an act of worship and a witness; it was not superstition. As the natives and the French did not speak a common language, Cartier chose the best nonverbal way he could to demonstrate the Christian faith.

The English no less than the French numbered believers in Christ among their explorers. In England the interest in evangelism was combined with opposition to the Roman Catholic Church. The English wanted to see the Protestant Reformed faith dominant in America. Explorer Humphrey Gilbert, writing to Queen Elizabeth I in 1577, stated that the King of Spain was the "chief maintainer of the Romish religion, enemy to all others that be not of the same religion." He went on to point out that the queen was the "chief head of the Church of Christ and so an enemy to the Church of Rome." Gilbert wanted to see aggressive action against Spanish colonies in the New World.[4] Before dismissing these words as emotional and lacking in Christian charity, remember the times in which they were penned. Catholic Spain was a very real threat to England. Only eleven years after Gilbert wrote these words, England would fight for her life (and win) against the Spanish Armada's invasion attempt.

Rules for life on board ship were also decidedly religious. Sir Martin Frobisher, English explorer of eastern Canada, is one example of a commander who set such rules for his men. Frobisher forbade swearing, card playing, and "filthy communication." He also ordered that Church of England services be conducted twice daily.[5] Can you imagine modern sailors living under regulations such as these? Yet these rules were not empty forms; they were a way of life.

The place names which the English gave to the New World also reflect their religion. For instance, John Davis, explorer of northern Canada, named the southernmost cape of Baffin Island's Cumberland Peninsula "Cape of God's Mercy." The name tells us something about Davis. It also tells us something of more recent men who have shortened its name to Cape Mercy, removing the name of God.[6]

One more explorer we shall look at is Sir Francis Drake. During the years 1577–1580, Drake became the first Englishman to sail around the globe. Among his supplies for the voyage were a number of Bibles and prayer books for the use of the crew. The performance of religious duties was strictly enforced by Drake. When there was danger, special times of prayer to God were held. Drake also tried to perform the work of a missionary. On the California coast, Drake had his men pray, read the Bible, and sing psalms in front of the Indians. While they did not understand English, the Indians sat "very attentively" during these times of worship. They especially seemed to enjoy the singing. In the words of Drake, "...Yea, they [the Indians] took such pleasure in our singing of Psalms that whensoever they resorted to us their first request was this '*Gnaah*', by which they entreated that we would sing."[7]

Perhaps the most dramatic answer to prayer on Drake's voyage took place in January 1579. At that time his ship, the *Golden Hind*, ran onto a shoal in the Pacific. While Drake did all he could by lightening the ship and manning the pumps, he also had his men call upon God. He ordered his men to prayer and had his chaplain administer the sacrament and preach to the men. Far from an unnecessary waste of time at a critical moment, these spiritual activities were a vital part of the effort to save the ship and lives of the crew. As a result of prayer and work, the ship floated free. Historian Louis B. Wright has used the adverb *miraculously* to describe the deliverance of the ship from the shoal.[8]

We ought to mention briefly some incidents of the heroism of the French in exploring the interior of America. While their influence on American history is small, their dedication to the cause of Christ should not be forgotten. The first Frenchmen to venture deeply inland were Jesuit missionaries. Like David Livingstone of a future generation, they combined their calling as missionaries with the exploration of a "new" continent.

Often these men lost their lives in their service of God, as did Father Isaac Joques. In 1642 his party was ambushed by the Iroquois Indians. Joques escaped, while other members of his company were captured. Desiring to be a comfort to his friends, he returned and gave himself up to the Indians. After being tortured, Joques was held as a slave. Following a year of slavery, Joques escaped and returned to France. There he requested permission to return to the Indians once again. He was sent back as the French ambassador to the Iroquois. The need for missionary work was highlighted by an incident with took place at this time. The Iroquois captured an Algonquin Indian woman, whom they sacrificed and ate, crying to their god of war, "Areskoui, to thee we burn this victim, feast on her flesh, and grant us new victories!"[9] As with the Aztecs, the American Indians were not "noble savages" defiled by the Europeans. They were cannibals. In fact, the America of the Indians was torn continually by wars and fighting. As Morison points out, "...apart from the Iroquois confederation, every North American Indian tribe was in a perpetual state of war with its neighbors."[10]

The Colonists That Couldn't

At the very end of Samuel Eliot Morison's book *The European Discovery of America—The Northern Voyages*, covering the years A.D. 500

18

to 1600, there is an interesting and important observation: "Thus the sixteenth century closed," wrote Morison, "without England or France having established a colony in North America. When the seventeenth century dawned on New Year's Day, 1601, not one Englishman was living in North America, unless some of the Roanoke planters were still alive or a few French fishermen had elected to spend the winter on the St. Lawrence."[11]

Do you understand how amazing this is? By 1600 the Spanish had an advanced empire in the making in Mexico and southward. By contrast, the English and French had...nothing! One cannot help but wonder why. Considering Europe's level of technical advancement, there had been vast numbers of voyages of exploration. There had also been many attempts at starting colonies. So we return to the simple question once again: Why?

Very simply, God did not allow America's east coast to be settled; in His providence, He was keeping it clear for English Protestants who would come to America to establish the kingdom of God on its shores. In the late twentieth century, Anglo-Saxon Protestants are made to feel guilty about their heritage and are badgered about sins committed long, long ago. Instead of seeing their past as a godly and great heritage, they are taught to see it as an evil. The fact is that God used the Indians, the weather, and even the sinfulness of the human heart to clear the way for British Protestants to settle America.

There were many colonial failures, attempts to settle America that did not work. The list of failures is a long one. How could so large a number of experienced men fail again and again?

The French explorer Verrazano was a man who knew his Bible and desired to see France probe deeper into America for the glory of God and country. Apparently this was not God's plan. For so able an explorer, there was an amazing failure in 1524 to discover major bays along the coast which could have been used by French settlers. Verrazano sailed up the coast from North Carolina to Maine and missed such major havens as the Chesapeake and Delaware bays. Morison comments, "his failure to take a good look at the mouth of the Hudson River is perhaps the greatest opportunity missed by any North American explorer."[13] More amazing still, the French government took no interest in the discoveries Verrazano did make. Verrazano's failure is surprising enough on its own, but it is only the opening scene of this story.

19

The Spanish got no further than the French. Spain made two attempts at about the same time to explore and colonize the American coast. First there was Estevan Gomez.[14] Gomez sailed as far north as Desert Island, Maine, in one instance actually sailing up the Penobscot River as far as the present-day city of Bangor. He then made his way south along the New England coast to Rhode Island, where he kidnapped some Indians for slaves. (The Spanish were disgusted with him for this when he got home. He was forced to liberate the Indians. Let us remember this early Christian hostility to slavery.) The Spanish government did nothing about the discoveries Gomez made, and like the French, passed up a great opportunity.

Our geography books would read differently had Spain followed up on Gomez's work. Gomez gave Spanish names to various places in New England: Rio de Bueno Madre was his name for the Kennebec River in Maine. Rio San Antonio was Gomez's name for the Merrimack River in Massachusetts. The most striking name change involves C. de las Arenas, none other than Cape Cod!

The next year, 1526, the Spanish attempted to establish a colony on the North Carolina coast.[15] This expedition, led by Luis Vasquez de Ayllon, was made up of five hundred men, women, children, and friars. After some difficulty in finding a suitable site, they settled near the present location of Wilmington, naming their colony San Miguel de Guadalupe. Everything seemed to go wrong. First of all, the local Indians were suspicious of the settlers and refused to supply food. As this bad feeling was caused by a previous slave raid, the Spanish had brought this difficulty upon themselves. The fact that the colonists were an undisciplined group also made a rod for their own back. Nature joined in to make life difficult. That year the cold weather settled in early, causing hardships. In addition there was malaria. After Ayllon's death in October, the demoralized colonists headed home to Santo Domingo.

It was not only the French and Spanish who had their problems. The early attempts on the part of English businessmen to colonize America had no success. The time had not yet arrived for English Christians to come to America.

Two attempts were made by the British to colonize Roanoke Island, North Carolina. The first, in 1585, saw a group of Englishmen—no women—settle there. The absence of women always indicated that what was being established was more a trading post than a colony. It indicated that no attempt to build a community based on family life was intended. Moreover, through their own foolishness, the Englishmen turned what were friendly Indians into hostile enemies, who then put Roanoke under siege. The settlers' food supplies were running out and a ship commanded by Sir Francis Drake paid an unexpected visit. The men took advantage of this call to evacuate the island. Two weeks later a supply ship landed on the island and, finding no one there, sailed away again. An English fleet, arriving a month later, also found the island empty. They discovered from an Indian whom they captured what had happened. After stationing eighteen men on the island, they left.[16]

In 1587, another party of would-be colonists arrived on Roanoke. This group was made up of eighty-nine men, seventeen women, and eleven children. The original idea was to pick up the eighteen men left on Roanoke and then sail on to Chesapeake Bay to settle. Arriving on the island, there was no trace of the men left there. At this point, the captain of the fleet dropped a bombshell. All the colonists were told to get off the ships and settle on Roanoke. He said that it was too late in the summer to go on to Chesapeake Bay and make a start there. The real reason had more to do with his desire to get his passengers off his ships. In any case, the colonists found themselves on Roanoke Island. To make a long story short, these settlers also behaved without wisdom and needlessly antagonized the Indians. This is the last information we have of the colony. War with Spain would prevent another expedition from arriving at the island until 1590.

When the next expedition arrived, it found the settlement abandoned. There were two clues to where the colonists had gone. Carved upon a tree were the letters CRO. There was another carving upon a post at the entrance to the settlement: CROATOAN. According to an arrangement with the colonists, if they had to leave for any reason, they were to leave a carved message of where they were going. If they left because of an emergency, they were to carve a Maltese cross next to their destination. As no such cross had been made, the settlers had evidently left peacefully. Croatoan Island was not very far away, and there were known to be friendly Indians there. Impossible as it is to believe, the newcomers never went to Croatoan Island to check. Part of the fleet went back to England, and the rest went raiding in the Caribbean Sea.

The most likely theory about the missing colonists is that they actually merged with the Indians on Croatoan. It is known that this tribe migrated inland to modern-day Roberson County. Proof for this theory is drawn from the existence of blue-eyed, fair-haired members of this tribe.

Twenty years before Roanoke, a more tragic story took place involving Huguenots, French Protestants. To escape Catholic persecution, in 1564 a group of Huguenots tried to set up a Protestant colony at Port Royal, South Carolina, on the St. Johns River, near present-day Jacksonville, Florida. King Philip II of Spain heard about this colony and was determined to wipe it out. As a Catholic, he did not want to see Protestants settle and organize into colonies in America. King Philip organized his own group of colonists under the leadership of Pedro Menedez de Aviles, with orders to destroy the Huguenots and set up a Spanish Catholic colony in its place. The next year Aviles landed at the site of St. Augustine, thirty-five miles to the south of Fort Caroline. There followed a battle in which the Protestants were nearly destroyed completely. On the gallows upon which Aviles executed many of the Huguenots he put these words: "I do this not to Frenchmen but to Lutherans."

Three years later Dominique de Gourgues, a French Huguenot and former Spanish galley slave, led an attack in revenge which annihilated the Spanish colony. The avenger left this inscription: "I do this not to Spaniards...but as to traitors, robbers, and murderers."[18] This is one of the most tragic stories of sixteenth-century America. We leave this incident without comment save for this: In the purposes of God, the Protestants who were to colonize America's eastern seaboard were to be British.

Yet another failure in attempts at colonization was led by Bartholomew Gosnold of England. This expedition was a commercial one, sailing from Cornwall to Cape Cod in 1602. The band that settled on an island just off the cape was made up of twenty men, no women, no families. The Indians made an unexplained attack on these men in which one of the Englishmen was wounded. Added to this setback was fighting among themselves over the distribution of supplies. In the end Gosnold lost control over this selfish group of men, and they sailed back to England.[19]

Three years later in 1605, French explorer Samuel de Champlain visited Massachusetts, discovering (or rediscovering) great harbors such as Boston and Plymouth. He then sailed north to Passamaquoddy Bay, Maine, where he tried to organize a settlement. The rugged coastline and bad weather combined to discourage this attempt.

The next year a Frenchman named DeMont tried three times to land on Cape Cod. Twice unfavorable winds drove him off. On the third attempt his ship was wrecked. Thus was his attempt to organize an agricultural colony defeated. Another Frenchman, Poutrincourt, tried to do the same thing and also suffered defeat on the rocks of Cape Cod.[20]

This record is truly amazing. Time after time attempts to establish permanent settlements failed. The reasons were different, even unrelated, but the results were always the same. From the few failures we have discussed, we have made this list of all the major reasons for defeat in the colonization of America. *Weather*: Ayllon, Champlain, DeMont, Poutrincourt. *Undisciplined colonists and/or leaders*: Ayllon, the two Roanoke settlements, and Gosnold. *Government indifference*: Verrazano and Gomez. *Indians*: Ayllon, Gosnold, and, after provocation, the two Roanoke settlements. *Geographical conditions*: Ayllon and Champlain. *Careless exploring*: Verrazano. *Illness*: Ayllon. Such a wide variety of problems affecting a wide variety of people in a wide variety of places shows more sign of pattern than of chance.

For a historian who does not believe in God, the facts in this chapter will have been put together in a most unscientific manner. But if you accept the fact of a God who controls history, the conclusion is obvious. The providence of God was at work. Moreover, all the factors which were most significant in preventing other colonies from surviving were present in the later successful colonies. There were also, however, remarkable circumstances which worked for their survival. The colonists who were there, and who suffered the adversities, saw in them as well as in the providential circumstances, the hand of God.

23

1. Samuel Eliot Morison, *The European Discovery of America—The Northern Voyages* (New York: Oxford University Press, 1971), p. 391.
2. Ibid., p. 313.
3. Ibid., pp. 370, 374–375.
4. Louis B. Wright, *Gold, Glory, and the Gospel* (New York: Atheneum Books, 1970), pp. 319–320.
5. Morison, *European Discovery*, p. 532
6. Ibid., p. 590.
7. Wright, *Gold, Glory, and the Gospel*, pp. 315, 336.
8. Ibid., pp. 336–337.
9. Peter Marshall and David Manuel, *The Light and the Glory* (Old Tappan, New Jersey: Fleming H. Revell Company, 1977), pp. 77–78.
10. Morison, *European Discovery*, p. 417.
11. Ibid., p. 678.
12. Ibid., chapter 9: "The Voyages of Verrazano," pp. 277–316.
13. Ibid., p. 316.
14. Ibid., pp. 326–331.
15. Ibid., 332–338.
16. Ibid., chapter 19: "The First Virginia Colony," pp. 617–651.
17. Ibid., chapter 20: "The Second Virginia Colony," pp. 656–679.
18. Wright, *Gold, Glory, and the Gospel*, p. 318.
19. Douglas Hill, *The English to New England* (New York: Clarkson N. Potter, 1975), pp. 3–4.
20. Tim J. Campbell, *Central Themes of American Life* (Grand Rapids: William B. Eerdmans, 1957), pp. 18–19.
21. Ibid., p. 19.

The Time Is Ripe

THREE

One fact should be obvious by now, namely that because the providence of God is here stressed, most scholarly historians will reject this as bad history at best. Sadly, all too many supposedly Christian historians, including church historians, would agree. For them, references to the providence of God, and a belief in God's governing, quieting, and correcting hand in history, are not "historical." For them, "good history" is naturalistic; it is written without reference to God, or to man's fall and sin, or to Christ as the only hope of men and nations. For us, what these men call "good history" is anti-Christian history and false. *To omit God's hand in history is to falsify every fact.* This perspective is a necessary one for Christians: to regard history from anything but a God-centered faith is a sin. It is to be guilty of what Paul condemns in Romans 1: it means that, professing themselves to be wise, such historians are fools who change the truth of God into a lie and worship and serve man, the creature, more than the Creator (Romans 1:22, 25). Let this perspective govern us here and in everyday life. We cannot have one kind of faith in the pulpit and home, and another in the writing of history.

It was 1607 when God's time finally came for the colonization of America's east coast. It was in that year that the settlement at Jamestown, Virginia, was established. While this settlement, which blossomed into the colony of Virginia, went through great hardships on the material level, the most difficult struggle was religious. The royal charter of the colony stated that "the world and services of God be preached, planted and used according to the rites and doctrines of the Church of England."[1]

This requirement of the charter was, in practice, good and bad. It was good in that the government of Virginia was legally charged with

25

maintaining the Christian faith in the colony. Unlike the little bands of traders who had tried to settle without a thought toward God, Virginia was commanded by the king to faithfully worship God.

And yet it was also bad, because the charter stated that God was to be worshiped according to the faith of the Church of England (known as the Episcopal Church in modern America). At that period of time, a great conflict was under way in England between the Anglicans (who supported a formal church with its prayer book and ceremonies) and the Puritans (Anglicans who felt that the prayer book ceremonies made the church too much like the Roman Catholic Church). This struggle was exported to Virginia, where it caused many problems.

At first, there was little difficulty. All the Anglican ministers who came to Virginia were Puritans and conducted their churches as they saw fit. There was no bishop in the colony to force the clergy to toe the line. Things changed, however, when Charles I became king of England in the 1620s. The king was a strong supporter of the Church of England and very opposed to the Puritans, and therefore many harsh steps were taken against the English Puritans, some of which were imitated in Virginia. The royal governor enforced the laws which insisted that the prayer book be used in all worship services and those who refused to conform were forced to leave the colony.

In England the Puritans in the Parliament revolted against the king. As the king began to lose the civil war which followed, increasingly harsher laws were imposed in Virginia. One law removed the duty of parishioners to financially support their minister in instances where he did not use the prayer book. This suppression lasted until Oliver Cromwell, the Puritan leader, became lord protector of England. Charles I was executed for treason on January 29, 1649. Two years later the Puritans took control of Virginia.

During this period, the Puritans had great liberty in Virginia. Virginia's religious character was formed along Puritan lines. When Charles II became king at the Restoration, the resulting prosecution of Puritans in Virginia was not successful. The Puritan faith was by then too deeply ingrained in the colony. Virginia would face the future with a religious faith that was emphatically Puritan.

The Pilgrims of Plymouth

We saw previously how God caused so many different things to work together to prevent the settlement of America. When the time was right, God performed even greater miracles to ensure the success of the English Christian settlers.

We all know something about the ever-appealing Pilgrims, a group of Christians who were so against the practices of the Church of England that they wanted to be entirely separate. In order to do this, after an interlude in Holland they ultimately had to sail for America in 1620. They put to sea in a small ship called the Mayflower.

One Pilgrim who lost heart at the last moment and stayed behind was Robert Cushman. Considering all the hardships of a small ship (followed by even worse conditions in America) which made their mission seemingly impossible, Cushman made a remark which was to prove ironic: "If we ever make a plantation," he wrote, "God works a miracle."[2] He was right. These were men mostly without practical experience in farming, building, and any kind of pioneering.

However, from the beginning God was with the Pilgrims. All the same, while God saved them from disaster, they were not delivered from the severest forms of afflictions. Due to many delays, the Pilgrims did not leave England until September 6, 1620. This late start meant arriving in America at the beginning of winter, the worst possible time to arrive, especially with nothing but wilderness to greet them. Still they set sail, and God went with them.

Late in the year the Atlantic can be very rough, as the Pilgrims discovered. Those many men, women, and children were cooped up below deck for weeks. Privacy and sanitation would have been impossible to maintain even if the ship had been still. As they tossed about on the sea, their condition was unbelievably bad.

One of the sailors had obviously taken a dislike to the Pilgrims and enjoyed tormenting them. As they huddled in their confined space, overcome with seasickness and all the other discomforts, this sailor would abuse them and tell them that they were going to die. He spoke also of his coming pleasure in throwing their bodies overboard! His pleasure in the misery of the Pilgrims was sadistic. Suddenly, however, this sailor became seriously ill and within a day was dead. Thus God showed the crew and the Pilgrims that these Christians were in His special care.[3] This was the way the Pilgrims saw his death. Shall we seek a purely naturalistic cause?

Although there was only one other death during the journey, a remarkable record for those days, there were close calls. God's protection can be seen in the case of a young lad named John Howland. In the middle of a storm, Howland foolishly went up on deck. As he reached the deck, the Mayflower pitched violently and Howland went over the side. This normally would have meant certain death. The Mayflower, however, had tipped so far over that the topsail halyards were in the water. Miraculously, although he went under the water, Howland managed to catch hold. Some of the crew had seen what happened and began pulling on the ropes. As the Mayflower righted herself, they were able to pull the boy safely on board. His rescue was a freak occurrence. The chances of Howland's being able to grab anything while being tossed about by the ocean were nonexistent. God was looking after His people.[4] This is the way the Pilgrims saw Howland's deliverance. Shall we call it chance?

On one occasion, the Pilgrims were able to save the Mayflower. During a storm, one of the main beams which supported the deck cracked. This could have meant disaster. Normally a ship would have nothing that would be able to rescue the situation, especially on a stormy sea. However, the Pilgrims had brought along just the thing to prop up the deck—a giant screw. History books disagree on just what this screw was meant to be used for. The two possibilities seem to be that it was just part of an old-fashioned printing press, or that it was meant to jack up the houses they were going to build. At any rate, this screw was placed under the beam to support it for the rest of the voyage. The unlikely presence of such a screw on board the ship, the critical circumstances, and the imaginative use of the screw again present us with an unusual situation.[5] Coincidence? Or providence?

The men who financed the Pilgrim expedition were not Christians. Through the years these backers were to take advantage of the Pilgrims in many ways. One serious problem they caused was the adding of passengers who were not particularly religious, let alone Pilgrims, to the Mayflower expedition. This nearly caused a crisis when they reached America.

After being at sea since the beginning of September, they sighted the tip of what is now Cape Cod on November 9. The Mayflower dropped anchor in Provincetown Harbor on the eleventh. At this point a difficulty arose. The charter which had been granted to the Pilgrims to set up a colony was valid for Virginia. Since the ship had landed outside Virginia's borders, some of the non-Pilgrim passengers thought it unnecessary to carry out their duties as listed in the charter and sought to be free of any control. To prevent anarchy, the Pilgrim leaders drew up the Mayflower Compact, which all the men were to sign before they went ashore, an important step for two reasons. First of all, as the Pilgrims were in the minority, if they failed to establish some form of civil government outside the original charter, control of the colony could have slipped from them. This would have meant that their intention of establishing the kingdom of God on American soil would have been lost before it ever began. Second, this document proves that from the beginning the government of Massachusetts had a religious basis. Indeed, the compact clearly says that the purpose of establishing the colony was "for the glory of God and advancement of the Christian faith, and honour of our King and countrie."⁶ The Pilgrims were not confusing Church and State. They were not recognizing the Church as ruler over the State. They were simply saying that God is King over both Church and State, as He is over families and individuals as well.

Many are under the impression that the Mayflower sailed up to Plymouth and the passengers disembarked on Plymouth Rock. The true story is quite different. After arriving at the tip of Cape Cod, everyone stayed on board ship, while expeditions were sent out to find a suitable place to found a colony. Immediately, we see God helping these Christians in many ways.

One expedition rowed ashore to get some firewood. During their walk along the shore, the men found an iron kettle filled with corn buried in the sand. What were the chances of their stumbling upon this? The fact is the Pilgrims were being looked after. The source of the pot? A French ship was wrecked in that bay three years before the Pilgrims arrived. The native Indians killed all but three of the survivors and kept the iron pot.⁷ If the settlers were blissfully unaware of the origins of the pot, they also did not know the Indians could no longer present a danger to them, as we shall see shortly.

There was also protection from youthful foolishness. While one of the exploring parties was ashore, a young Francis Billington, rummaging among his dad's belongings, found some gunpowder, which he began to play with. On a wooden ship, with a barrel of gunpowder beside him, he fired off three charges of powder from some of the firearms which were close by, and under normal circumstances ought to have blown the ship sky high. However, nothing happened and no one was injured, although we assume that young Francis's backside was warmed by his father.

The Pilgrims finally arrived at Plymouth on December 11. Well into the winter, they all lived on the Mayflower while shelters were being built. Food was scarce, the weather cold. It was not a harsh winter, which probably saved the colony. However, the stamina of the people was low. With poor living conditions and low rations of food, diseases such as scurvy and pneumonia struck hard. A total of forty-four passengers, half their number, died between December 1620 and March 1621, an average of 2.75 people per day. In the same period, roughly half the crew also died. Of those who did not die, most were ill.[8]

The Puritans lovingly cared for the sick, not only those of their own number but also those of the other colonists and crew. One crew member, who hated the Christians and would roundly curse them, fell ill; he received their attentive care. Repenting of his hateful attitude, he said, "Oh, you, I now see, show your love like Christians indeed one to another, but we let one another lie and die like dogs."[9]

It seemed as if the end of these settlers was only a matter of time. At a critical moment an Indian walked boldly into their settlement and spoke to them in English. After the colonists had given him a small meal, he began to tell his story. His name was Samoset. He had learned English from traders and fishermen on the coast of Maine where he lived. Apparently he liked to travel, as he had "hitched" a ride down the coast to Cape Cod from an English sea captain. The Plymouth area had been the home of a fierce tribe of Indians called the Patuxet, a tribe which killed every white man who landed on that shore. Only a couple of years or so before the Pilgrims landed, a great plague had broken out, and the entire tribe had been obliterated. The Pilgrims had planned to land in the South; they landed instead in the North, by "accident," but a safe place had been their "chance" harbor.[10] Again, was this chance or providence?

Samoset stayed the night and then left. Through his diplomatic activities, Massasoit, chief of the Wampanoag tribe, paid a state visit to Plymouth shortly after. This tribe, now that the Patuxets were no more, was the closest neighbor, fifty miles to the southwest of the Pilgrims. The two peoples had a very friendly meeting and became allies and trading partners. But for the Pilgrims the greatest blessing of the day was to meet a very well-traveled Indian named Squanto.

Squanto also spoke English fluently. His story is yet another showing how circumstances helped the settlers. Squanto had been a member of the fierce Patuxet tribe. In 1605, he had been taken to England by one of the explorers. It was there that he learned English. He returned to

America as interpreter for Captain John Smith in 1614. He was taken prisoner along with some other Indians by the captain of one of Smith's ships and sold in the Málaga slave market in Spain. He became a servant in a religious institution of some kind there for a while. He was able to get away and to reach London, where he lived with a merchant. This merchant loaned him as an interpreter to a man sailing to Newfoundland who, in turn, lent him to a sea captain sailing to New England. He was either released or jumped ship at this point and made his way back to the land of his native Patuxet tribe. To his horror, the tribesmen were all dead, killed by a plague. He had little real choice but to join with Massasoit and the Wampanoags. And at that point he met the Pilgrims, thanks to a "tourist" named Samoset. Squanto's route to the Pilgrims was a roundabout one: New England, England, New England, Spain, England, Newfoundland, and finally, New England. This Indian was prepared, and in the right place at the right time, to give the Pilgrims invaluable help. Was this coincidence? The Pilgrims were not foolish enough to think so. In the words of Plymouth's Governor Bradford, Squanto was "a special instrument of God for their good."[11] He was able to show the settlers how to get the best out of Cape Cod's agriculture, hunting, and fishing, and this knowledge probably saved the colony from starvation.

One of the interesting features of the Plymouth Colony was its experiment with socialism. At the beginning of its history there was no private property in the colony, because everything belonged to the merchant company. The effects of socialism then, as now, were uniformly bad. For one thing, productivity in growing food was not as high as it should have been; for another, socialism bred bad feelings. Bachelors disliked working for other men's wives and children. In the same way, married women had no desire to cook, wash, and mend clothes for the bachelors. Recognizing this problem, the leaders of Plymouth showed their good sense and flexibility. Every family was given a field in which to grow their own food. The result of this step is recorded by Governor Bradford for us. Allowing families to work for themselves "made all hands very industrious...the women now went willingly into the field and took their little ones with them to set corn."[12]

Through all the work of organizing their colony, God was with them every step of the way. In 1623, there was a drought during the growing season which threatened the harvest. Plymouth held a "solemn day of humiliation" in which the colonists prayed to God to send rain. No sooner had they done this than the clouds gathered and it rained, not a downpour which would have flattened the crop but gentle showers of rain which saved them from disaster.[13] Even the Indians saw this as an act of God and became more responsive to the Christian witness and ways of the Pilgrims.

Often, the legal system of Pilgrim and Puritan New England has come under attack, wrongly so. Pilgrim justice shall be considered later. Regarding the Pilgrims, Morison writes, "For humanity, the Colony of New Plymouth was well in advance of its era. It never used torture, or burned criminals alive, or punished an alleged witch, or applied any of the cruel punishments which were then common in civilized countries."[14]

History of the Puritans

The Puritans were another group of Anglicans whose beliefs were almost identical with those of the Pilgrims. The major difference was in their attitude toward the Church of England. The Pilgrims saw no hope of reforming the Anglican Church and wanted to sever relations, whereas the Puritans desired to remain Anglicans and alter the system from within. While the Pilgrims in theory were more extreme than the Puritans, the Puritan life-style was by far the more severe of the two. On the other hand, the latter were more moderate than modern myth would have us believe.

In the late 1620s, the first Puritans landed in what would become the Massachusetts Bay Colony. The territory of this colony was roughly the land of the present state of Massachusetts, except for Cape Cod, which formed the Plymouth Colony. The Puritans came in far larger numbers than the Pilgrims; they also had much more money to finance their colony.

For all their advantages, the first winter they saw much sickness and death, similar to the Pilgrims' first winter. Puritan Governor Endicott appealed to Governor Bradford at Plymouth for assistance. Bradford was very generous, sending Plymouth's own doctor, Samuel Fuller, to its sister colony. Dr. Fuller worked all winter long, helping the Massachusetts Bay colonists in their difficulties. His labor helped give the Puritans more respect for their Pilgrim neighbors, whom they tended to think were rather odd.

Doctor Fuller also had a personal influence on Endicott, talking much during that winter about the Plymouth Colony and its character. Dr. Fuller, a deacon at Plymouth, explained the church structure and government of the colony. This impressed Endicott, who decided that, while remaining Anglican, his colony ought to have its church set up in a like manner. This required the church to have three officers: a pastor, a teacher, and a ruling elder, all elected by the church membership.[15]

Endicott acted as governor until John Winthrop arrived from England. Winthrop arrived in 1629 with several ships, bringing more supplies and colonists. On their voyage across the ocean, the travelers received many sermons. When it was the turn of Governor Winthrop's son Henry to preach, he gave a stirring message; it has come down to us because of the often-quoted phrase about "a city upon a hill." Politicians and statesmen have often cited that statement since then. However, put in its context, Winthrop's point tells us that the Puritans saw the meaning of their experiment. "We shall be as a *city upon a hill*, the eyes of all people are upon us; so that if we shall deal falsely with our God in this work we have undertaken and so cause Him to withdraw His present help from us, we shall be made a story and a byword through the world."[16]

As with the Pilgrims, it is obvious that God was determined to make the Puritan settlement a success. The following are a few of the amazing things that happened in the colony.

Cotton Mather, a famous preacher, tells of a carpenter who was building a house. "While the builder was above, working on the beams, several children were below him sitting in a circle. Suddenly, by accident, a heavy beam fell down directly above the children. The man just had time enough to shout a prayer, 'Oh, Lord, direct,' and the beam landed on its end in the center of the circle of children and then fell over between two of them. No one was injured."[17]

Another incident involved Governor Winthrop's wife and two young daughters. His daughters were sitting under a large pile of logs plucking the feathers off some birds. The feathers were blowing into their house, so Mrs. Winthrop came out and told them to move somewhere else. No sooner had they moved than the log pile collapsed onto the spot where they had been. Had God not directed the wind and feathers, had Mrs. Winthrop been slower in telling her daughters to move away, the results would have been tragic.[18]

Governor Winthrop also told a story about caterpillars, which apparently fell in a thunderstorm in 1646. Winthrop says the ground was bare of them before the storm, and afterward they covered the ground and began to eat all the vegetation. Around the colony, a day of humiliation and prayer was held, and the caterpillars vanished as quickly as they came.[19]

Perhaps the most dramatic event involved an invasion attempt by the French. A French fleet from Nova Scotia was sailing toward New England with forty ships of war under the command of the Duke D'Anville. The churches of New England declared a day of fasting and prayer. It was a perfectly clear day when the people met for prayer. In the Old South Church in Boston, the time of prayer was interrupted by gusts of strong wind which had seemingly blown up from nowhere. This answer to prayer rattled the window panes of that church even as its people were asking for deliverance. And this storm did deliver them. The French fleet was wrecked in the storm. The duke and his chief general committed suicide.[20] Puritan accounts cite many providential incidents to illustrate the faith that God cares for His own.

Attending church and listening to semons played a very large part in the life of the colony. One had no choice on Sundays; to attend the morning and afternoon services was required, but most colonists wanted even more, so that limits on the number of services were set. Aside from the Puritan faithful who went to worship God, the rest of the community also had an interest in church. It was the "entertainment" of the week, and the gathering together of the whole community. Sermons were full of illustrations drawn from everyday life. Preachers were also expected to be informed on current events, to comment on the news, applying biblical observations to the latest events. Congregations brought paper and ink with them to church in order to make notes on the sermon because a church service was for them both education and worship.

There was also a sermon one evening during the week. Attendance was not required, but the colony tried to regularize the time, the same night in all towns, to prevent too much time spent traveling to various towns to hear yet another sermon. In terms of today's standards, this was a strange problem. However, this practice was causing a lack of productivity since people were out traveling the countryside to attend services instead of working. By having all the meetings the same night, the problem was solved.[21] The Puritan work ethic was important, but the hunger for biblical knowledge was greater.

One of the interesting institutions of Puritan church life was the Tithing-Man who, during church services, would stand watching the congregation with a staff in his hand. On one end of the staff was a feather, on the other a round knob. If anyone was about to doze off, the Tithing-Man would take action. The ladies would have their faces tickled gently by the feather, the gentlemen would be tapped by the knob! The Tithing-Man, however, was not forced on a suffering congregation; he was no religious version of "big brother is watching you." The congregations were anxious to hear the sermons. The distance to the church was sometimes a good walk, and a tiring one. The Puritans knew that the flesh is weak; against their best efforts they might fall asleep and miss part of the sermon. For this reason, the congregation paid the Tithing-Man themselves to make sure they were kept awake. To interpret such things from our perspective is to misunderstand the Puritans.

Knowing that this was a society where God was at the center of day-to-day life, it is no surprise to learn that the same was true of their legal system. The laws of the colony were based on the Law of God as found in the Bible. One example of this was the laws regarding Sunday. Sunday, referred to as the Sabbath after the Old Testament day of rest, was a special day. On that day all work and pleasure came to a stop. Following the practice of the Jews, the Puritans began their Sabbath at 6:00 P.M., Saturday night. This followed the Jewish practice of limiting the distance one could go on the Sabbath to what was called a "Sabbath Day's Journey."[22]

Although they were loyal subjects of the British Crown, their first loyalty was to God; God was the true King over all the earth, they believed. Therefore, they were bound to obey His commands as found in the Bible.[23]

Moral crimes were also handled according to God's Law. In 1642, a teenager named Thomas Granger was found guilty of bestiality. The authorities did not act rashly. They took advice on the matter and then acted according to Leviticus 20:15, 16. On the eighth of September, the animals (a mare, a cow, two goats, five sheep, two calves, and a turkey) were killed in front of him. Afterward, Granger himself was put to death. By this incident we see that the Puritans felt it their duty to uphold all of the biblical law.[24]

However, we must not dwell only upon the harsh side of Puritan justice. Often, those who confessed their guilt and repented would find that the Puritan justices were ready to give guidance and pastoral care. Marshall and Manuel cite the case of Tyral Pore. This young girl was brought before the Middlesex County Court in 1656, where she broke down and confessed her guilt with a humble spirit. Upon her sorrow for her sins, the magistrates were prepared to forgive her. "The Puritan magistrates, whose law book was the Bible, were generally far more anxious to see a sinner come to repentance than to mete out punishment."[25]

There were laws on the statute books besides those concerned with crime and punishment. One such law dealt with the education of children. In our day the State is claiming with progressive boldness that it, the great provider of the people's welfare, is the only institution which should be allowed to educate the children. The State dislikes private education of all kinds, but especially those "private" schools which teach the children from a Christian standpoint, thus impeding the State's desire to indoctrinate the youth with secular humanism, life without God. In the 1640s, the Massachusetts Bay Colony passed laws requiring parents and apprentice-masters to teach their charges to read, to understand the Christian religion, and to know the laws which governed their colony. They saw, in the case of parents, the failure to educate one's children as in the same class of neglect as failure to feed, clothe, or house them. These laws also commanded every village with a population over fifty to appoint someone to teach the local children reading and writing.[26] The purpose of this education was to allow the children to read the Bible and to study their religious faith. Schooling was seen as an aid to the Church's work, as Christian in nature, not as something to be divorced from the faith.

With hindsight, from this frame of reference we can see that public funding for education was an error. It must be remembered that these leaders saw the colony as the kingdom of God on earth. They gave the State too much power, because it seemed impossible that godless men could ever take control. The worst example of Puritan public funding of education was Harvard University. The New England Confederation, a loose United Nations type alliance of the colonies, took control of Harvard in 1644. Each family in New England was to pay a shilling, a shilling's worth of wampum (Indian money made from seashells), or a quarter bushel of wheat.[27] The motives behind this were praiseworthy, but the results, even at the time, were not always as good as one might wish. As Kate Caffrey has observed, "Harvard based itself solidly on the classics. Those who disapproved of this pagan foundation showed themselves madly anti-collegiate, vociferously protesting until it was put to them that they would be far better off in Rhode Island."[28] The problem with the Puritans was not religious fanaticism but an underground secularism.

Plymouth, relying on education in the home, did not set up a school until 1671, fifty-one years after the colony was founded. The next year the colonists hired a schoolmaster named Anmi Ruhmah Corlet, a Harvard graduate. Like his alma mater, he was based solidly on classics. This did not suit the Plymouth people, who were more interested in their children learning reading, writing, and arithmetic. Corlet refused to become more practical and down to earth, and therefore left.[29]

Kate Caffrey, whether she knew it or not, showed the power of education at home while praising New England's state education for girls, writing:

From the beginning girls' education was regarded as important; it is to the greatest credit of New England that its citizens realized so soon the truth of Mrs. Pandit's noble dictum that if you educate a boy you educate a man, but if you educate a girl you educate a family. Cotton Mather's daughter Katharine learned Latin and Greek; George Wythe's mother taught her son Greek.[30]

The home was seen as the basic school:

Families became little cells of righteousness where the mother and father disciplined not only their children but also their servants and any boarders they might take in. In order that no one should escape this wholesome control, it was forbidden for anyone to live alone; unmarried men and maids were required to place themselves in some family if their own had been left behind. Parents were obliged to take care that all their children and apprentices learned to read, so that everyone would be able to see for himself in the Bible what opportunities for salvation God offered to man and what sins he forbade.[31]

Why then did education pass from a family affair to a State-imposed and financed one during the second generation of colonists? Marshall and Manuel pinpointed the answer in a chapter of their book called "God's Controversy with New England."[32] While the second-genera-

37

tion Puritans were still a religious, God-fearing people, their Christianity was not as powerful as that of their parents. They were becoming settled and, they thought, not as totally dependent on God's care. As Mather put it, "Religion begat prosperity, and the daughter devoured the mother."[33]

Another result of the cooling interest in religion was the "halfway covenant."[34] Simply put, the problem was this: many of the baptized children of the original settlers never became converted Christians, although they remained somewhat religious. This means that their children in turn could not be baptized. The Puritans' theology of the covenant held that God entered into a covenant of grace with believers. They would trust Jesus Christ for the forgiveness of their sins and seek to obey His Law and God would save them. This covenant extended to the children of believers as well, unless upon reaching adulthood they chose not to participate in it. The Puritans believed that as Christians obeyed the Gospel, their offspring would, in time, be the Lord's as well. Because of this, they had their children baptized as a seal, or a mark, of the covenant.

In terms of Scripture, no unconverted person could have his children baptized, as the pastors well knew. On the other hand, not to baptize their children meant that the Church would lose its influence and central role in society. The answer was the halfway covenant. Reduced to basics, this measure allowed baptized people, though not converted, to have a partial membership in the Church. This would allow their children to be baptized but would not permit them to take communion. It was a halfway covenant for halfway committed "Christians."[35]

This halfway covenant caused great disagreement. Most of the clergy favored it because if the children were not allowed to be baptized, the people who were not true believers would drift away from the Church. The laity, however, were against it. Church membership was an important matter. For one thing, one of the qualifications to vote in civil elections was church membership. The halfway covenant would allow unconverted people to share control over the colony's affairs. This proposal, after all the arguments, passed into law, a sad day for the Church. As one writer put it, "Thus although the churches were assured of permanent place in the community, they had to be content with an increasing number of those who were to all appearances devoid of any interest in the gospel message."[36]

We see how the halfway covenant threatened another colonial institution, the Freemen. This was a group made up of the men of the colony who were of age, members of the Church, and not servants or slaves. It was this group who elected the governor, lieutenant governor, and deputies (members of the legislature). This group was the natural aristocracy of Massachusetts Bay. Because of the qualifications to be met, Governor Winthrop believed that the colony had not established a democracy. Only those men, mainly heads of families who had proven themselves to be both religious and responsible, had this right of leadership. Plymouth had its Freemen as well. There, however, the qualifications were stricter. Plymouth's Freemen, unlike those of Massachusetts, were a minority of the men of the colony. Far from settling a small point of church order, the halfway covenant threatened to make it easier to have a watered-down group of Freemen; the church-membership requirement would be easier to fulfill, thus endangering the spiritual quality of the group. The slide from enlightened spiritual government to common democracy had begun.[37]

Another important step taken by both Plymouth and Massachusetts Bay was the drawing up of a "bill of rights." This was a statement of the legal rights of the citizens and the form of justice to be enjoyed in the colony. These documents were similar to England's Magna Charta and the United States Constitution's first ten amendments.

Plymouth's "bill of rights" was called the General Fundamentals and became law in 1636. This document set forth such important rights as trial by jury. While not setting forth a particular system of government, it did set up the principles that were to guide it. One provision, the significance of which we shall see later, was for the encouragement and protection of Congregational churches; the towns were to provide support for their Congregational ministers.[38]

Massachusetts Bay's Body of Liberties was a document similar to the General Fundamentals. This document did cause a measure of controversy before becoming law in 1641. Governor Winthrop was against it; his major reason was that it would create difficulties with the colonial charter. A provision of the charter said that the colony could not pass laws that went against those of England. If the colony were to make laws according to the Bible, they would certainly be different from those of England. Winthrop favored the method of allowing the judges to make rulings based on existing laws. These decisions, which would be biblical, could be used as legal precedents by which the colony would have to abide. But, as they would not be new laws as such, there would be no trouble about the charter.

Unlike the General Fundamentals, the Body of Liberties set up a system of local government which was quite unique. The document stated that each town would be governed by "select persons" elected each year by the local Freemen. This number, not more than nine, would then govern the town.[39]

There is another aspect of Massachusetts government which shows how important the Church was. This involves land and settlements. Elsewhere in the American colonies, various individuals would be granted tracts of land to settle. This was not the case in New England. Usually, a group of colonists would come together and form a church. After this was established, they would go to the legislature of the Massachusetts Bay and ask for a grant of land for a new township. The group would then, as a church, receive the land. The settlers would set out land for the church, village green, and other lots for public purposes. The rest of the land would be divided between the members of the church.

This system had many interesting results in village life. For one thing, it made it less likely that fundamental religious differences would arise. As all the original settlers were also members of a new parish church, no land would be available for newcomers unless the original inhabitants sold out. This church-centered system also helped the church keep discipline among its members. The worst punishment the church could inflict (as opposed to the town's civil government, which was separate) was excommunication, stripping a person of his membership. This would not cause him to lose his land but it would make him a social outcast. In our time, a man thrown out of one church will simply join another. But, back in colonial days, especially in a new settlement, there was only one church, and all the townspeople were members. If church members failed to behave according to the Bible, life could become very lonely.[40]

Roger Williams

It would be wrong to think that all the Christians in the New England of the seventeenth century agreed on all the religious issues of the day. The Puritans felt they had a real problem on their hands, having to deal with folk like the Quakers and the Baptists, who were not interested in having anything to do with their churches.

The most famous religious individualist was Roger Williams. Williams arrived in the Massachusetts Bay Colony in February 1631. From the very beginning, he proclaimed to all who would listen his belief that the Church of Christ must be pure. This, however, was the Puritan position as well, as their name indicates. But Roger Williams took his ideas of purity to extremes.

Williams disagreed with the Puritan policy of trying to purify the Church of England by staying within it. He finally left for the Plymouth Colony to join with the real separatists. Williams turned against Plymouth when he heard the news that the colony's agents in London attended Anglican worship services. He demanded, if these men failed to repent, that Plymouth should excommunicate them. After only two years in the Plymouth Colony, he left because of this issue.[41]

One fact about Williams that makes his case so sad is that he was a very likable man. Both Governor Bradford of Plymouth and Governor Winthrop of Massachusetts retained their friendship with Williams. Winthrop in particular corresponded with Williams throughout his life. These men disagreed strongly, but in a godly manner.

When Williams left Plymouth, members of the church at Salem invited him to become their minister. There, with a pulpit of his own, his observations became more and more extreme. He called the king a liar, and held that the king had no right to grant the colony a charter because the land had belonged to the Indians and not to the Crown. He preached that the Massachusetts Bay Colony ought to send its charter back to the king. The colony was willing to tolerate Williams and his beliefs; what the people could not allow was his openly preaching such dangerous views which would endanger the existence of the colony.

The colony took action and Williams was banished. Since it was winter, the authorities told Williams he could stay until spring, provided he kept his views to himself, which he refused to do.[42] The authorities then decided that Williams would have to be arrested and sent back to England. Governor Winthrop very kindly gave Williams a secret warning of what was being planned. He left immediately and fled to the Narragansett region, where he was to found the Colony of Providence.[43]

For all his fearless preaching against the king and the Massachusetts Bay Charter, Williams now went to England, where he asked for and received a charter for his new colony. He was starting to become more moderate.[44] However, Williams established his colony on his belief in the absolute separation of Church and State. Under this belief, the State could not act against anyone for his religious beliefs. This principle, of which Williams was one of the first supporters, was to play a vital role in shaping the nature of the American government down to this present day.

In Providence, however, this concept was to prove uncomfortable for him. All sorts of religious oddities and crackpots came flocking to Providence, where they would find peace from their persecutors in the other colonies. Williams, who found them very irritating, could do nothing about them. State was separate from Church. He had insisted on it; he would now have to live with it.

At first, in his zeal for purity, he kept narrowing himself down until he would have communion only with his wife. Then, finally realizing that absolute purity was impossible, he reversed himself and was ready to be open to everyone. Williams was not given to moderation, but at least his harsh exclusiveness was being broken down. He became a friend of the hostile Narragansett Indians and a warm personal friend of their chief. Many of these Indians were born again through his ministry.[46] This friendship proved very useful. In 1638, four Englishmen robbed and mortally wounded a Narragansett Indian. This Indian managed to crawl back to his people. As he lay dying, he identified the men who had committed the crime. Enraged, the Indians went to Williams and told him unless he saw that justice was done, and quickly, the Narragansetts would go on the warpath in revenge. Williams did not wait. He visited the Indian camp immediately to hear the story from the victim before he died. Williams captured the killers and turned them over to the Plymouth authorities. After a trial, the murderers were put to death in the presence of a delegation of Indians who were then satisfied that justice had been done. To his everlasting credit, Williams averted a bloody Indian uprising.[47]

The Later History of Seventeenth-Century New England

As the 1600s progressed, life became easier in the colonies. And, as we noted, the colonists' devotion to God became less strong. Marshall and Manuel, in their book *The Light and the Glory*, point out two judgments of God upon New England.[50]

The first judgment was King Philip's War. This war against the English was led by an Indian who was called "King Philip" by the colonists. This Indian was the son of Massasoit, who had been a close friend of the Pilgrims. Although this war against the settlers lasted only a little more than a year, a higher proportion of men were killed at that time than in any other war in American history.

This was not without its providential circumstances where the faith was still strong. Brookfield, Massachusetts was so spared.

On another occasion, the Indians chose to attack and burn the village of Sudbury and to leave the nearby village of Concord alone. Why? The Indians were frightened by Concord's godly minister, Edward Bulkely. According to an Indian account, the Indians said, "We no prosper if we burn Concord. The Great Spirit love that people. He tell us not to go there. They have a great man there. He pray."[51] God looks after his own.

This war was devastating. It pushed the frontier settlements back toward the coast and set back colonial advancement by many years.

The second judgment of God on New England is one we must deal with very carefully. The witchcraft trials lasted from May to October of 1692. Only twenty people were executed as witches, compared with hundreds killed in Europe the same year. It was the ministers of the colony who asked the governor to stop the witchcraft trials. Far from being witch-hunters, they realized that innocent people as well as the guilty were being brought to trial. In fact, one judge in the trials, Samuel Sewall, repented in public of his part in the affair.

The great disaster of the trials was the shift in emphasis. From a joyful work of establishing God's rule in a new land, the Puritans had moved to a task of negation, failing to recognize that the best offense against the fallen world is the Gospel and its saving power.

We began by calling attention to history as God's providential work. This is, after all, history as we read it in the Old Testament and the New. The Book of Acts stops without a conclusion, perhaps to tell us that the history of Christ's work through His servants continues. This was how the Pilgrims and Puritans saw their history. It is necessary that we see our world and our lives in like terms. Only then can we know the providence of God.

1. Ernest T. Thompson, *Presbyterians in the South* (Atlanta: John Knox Press, 1973), p. 11.
2. Samuel Eliot Morison, *The Story of the "Old Colony" of New Plymouth* (New York: Alfred A. Knopf, 1956), p. 24.
3. Peter Marshall and David Manuel, *The Light and the Glory* (Old Tappan, New Jersey: Fleming H. Revell Company, 1977), p. 117.
4. Kate Caffrey, *The Mayflower* (New York: Stein and Day, 1974), p. 108.
5. Morison, *New Plymouth*, p. 37–38.
6. Caffrey, *Mayflower*, p. 132.
7. Morison, *New Plymouth*, p. 50; Marshall and Manuel, *Light and the Glory*, pp. 112–123.
8. Caffrey, *Mayflower*, pp. 112–123.
9. Ibid., p. 135.
10. Marshall and Manuel, *Light and the Glory*, pp. 129–131.
11. Morison, *New Plymouth*, p. 70.
12. Ibid., p. 95.
13. Ibid., p. 97.
14. Ibid., p. 163.
15. Marshall and Manuel, *Light and the Glory*, pp. 162–163.
16. Caffrey, *Mayflower*, p. 229.
17. Marshall and Manuel, *Light and the Glory*, p. 210.
18. Ibid., p. 210.
19. Ibid., pp. 217–218.
20. Caffrey, *Mayflower*, pp. 278–279.
21. Marshall and Manuel, *Light and the Glory*, pp. 186–187.
22. Caffrey, *Mayflower*, p. 281.
23. Ibid., p. 301.
24. Ibid., pp. 268–269.
25. Marshall and Manuel, *Light and the Glory*, pp. 172–173.
26. Caffrey, *Mayflower*, pp. 289–290; *Presbyterians in America* (New York: Viking Press, 1973), p. 161; Edmund S. Morgan, *The Puritan Dilemma* (Boston: Little, Brown, 1958), pp. 71, 173.
27. Caffrey, *Mayflower*, p. 296.
28. Ibid., pp. 296–297.
29. Ibid., pp. 290–291.
30. Ibid., p. 290.
31. Marshall and Manuel, *Light and the Glory*, p. 183.
32. Ibid., p. 209–219.
33. Peter Y. DeJong, *The Covenant Idea in New England Theology* (Grand

Rapids: Eerdmans, 1945). Chapter 5, pp. 110–122, gives a full discussion of the halfway covenant.

34. Claerence L. Ver Steeg, *The Formative Years* (New York: Hill and Want, 1964), pp. 85–87.
35. Marshall and Manuel, *Light and the Glory*, p. 220.
36. DeJong, *Covenant Idea*, p. 121.
37. Ver Steeg, *Formative Years*, p. 41.
38. Morison, *New Plymouth*, pp. 152–153.
39. Morgan, *Puritan Dilemma*, pp. 166–173 for a full discussion of the General Fundamentals.
40. Marshall and Manuel, *Light and the Glory*, p. 173.
41. Ibid., pp. 194–195; Morgan, *Puritan Dilemma*, p. 120.
42. Marshall and Manuel, *Light and the Glory*, pp. 195–196.
43. Ver Steeg, *Covenant Idea*, pp. 48–49; Morgan, *Puritan Dilemma*, pp. 128–192.
44. Marshall and Manuel, *Light and the Glory*, pp. 196–197.
45. Ibid., p. 199.
46. Ibid., pp. 197–198.
47. Morison, *New Plymouth*, p. 212; Caffrey, *Mayflower*, pp. 266–267.
48. Morison, *New Plymouth*, p. 271.
49. Ibid., p. 284.
50. Marshall and Manuel, *Light and the Glory*, pp. 223–239.
51. Ibid., p. 228.

Puritan Law and Growing Secularism

FOUR

History gives us a variety of changes and circumstances, but it also has its constant factors. One of these constants is that every individual is a sinner apart from Jesus Christ. Moreover, even the saved man is by no means perfectly sanctified in this life. As a result, history often repeats itself because fallen man insists on repeating his sins.

We should not be surprised, therefore, that colonial Americans in the early 1700s were upset over inflation. The colonies were issuing paper money, which quickly lost its value. In foreign affairs, British mercantilism led to protectionism: the effort to sell British goods to foreign countries and the colonies while refusing to allow foreigners to sell to Britain and her colonies. The premise "Buy British" was unpopular with Americans who could get cheaper goods from France, Spain, and elsewhere, and it threatened colonial prosperity.

Having had a general look at the concerns of the American colonies in previous chapters, we can now proceed to investigate the way of life in the colonies.

The Indians

Many emotional reports have been written about the way the English treated the Indians. All too many writers seek to impose guilt feelings on contemporary Americans for the sins of past men we had no relationship to. The truth of colonial and Indian contacts is often obscured.

The Puritans were suspicious and somewhat afraid of the Indians. We can grant, too, that some settlers felt Indians had more in common with the beasts than with humans. Some felt that Indians were, as complete pagans, the allies of the devil. At one point, Roger Williams, commenting on a war with the Pequot Indians, said that these Indians were not afraid of the Puritan militia because the Pequot expected help from Satan.[1]

Even John Eliot, missionary to the Indians, expressed caution. He was certain that these natives were not to be trusted. He went so far as to say that some of the "praying Indians" were not really converted; in his words, they were "lost and falce." Until they proved themselves, they needed to be handled with care.[2] The Puritans believed that fallen man is a dangerous man. The Puritans faced the Indians sometimes as enemies. They lived in the knowledge of the sometimes savage customs of Indians, such as slavery and cannibalism.[3]

One of the accusations made against the settlers on behalf of the Indians involved land. The English stand accused of stealing land belonging to the Indians and using it for themselves. In order to determine whether or not the Indians really had any settled territory in the first place, we have to consider their way of life. The Indians, however, were largely nomadic, given to using any area where they could supplant other tribes. Some tribes did farming, but again with moves to new clearings and new hunting and fishing sites. They also raided other nomadic Indian bands. Solidarity or unity were not ideas they would have understood.[4] Nomadic tribes do not own land as we understand it. The only sense in which they might be said to have had land would be to say that everywhere they wandered was theirs, until they met another nomadic tribe; conflict then settled possession.

The whole question of whether or not the English took the Indians' land is a curious one. Down through history, countless numbers of people have taken land by force. John Greenway gives a sarcastic account of land ownership in Great Britain. If those of us who are English descendants did give America back to the Indians, where would we go? This is Greenway's answer: "Back to England to recover our erstwhile home from the descendants of the sixty thousand French thieves who landed with William the Conqueror at Senlac. Before the Normans there were the Germanic Anglo-Saxons who illegally took England from the Romanized Celts who had some of it from the blue-bottomed Picts who had it from the Bell Beaker people, whoever they were, and so on back to the Australopithecines who, if they existed in the scepter'd isle, would have delighted to sell it all over again for bananas."⁵ In brief, the entire world is stolen property several times over. This is not to justify the past. It is to set the record straight. Men cannot change the past; they can shape their present and future lives.

Moreover, the subject of land gives us an example of how Indian rights were respected under Puritan law. Although the Indians were disliked and feared by the settlers, colonial law still gave them justice. Massachusetts statutes stated that if an Indian claimed a piece of land was his, the white man would have to buy it from him; possession itself was not enough.⁶

Another instance of the protection of an Indian's rights occurred in a Boston court in 1672. Jonathan Atherton was found guilty of wounding an Indian with his sword. Atherton was forced to pay all expenses during the Indian's recovery and was not permitted to wear his sword in the colony until given permission by the court.⁷

Perhaps the most interesting instance of a concern over Indian rights involved firearms. During an Indian war scare in 1642, the Puritans confiscated all the Indians' guns that they could seize. Afterward, the colony voted to return the guns to the Indians, despite a general reluctance, because the Puritans realized that they had no legal right to these weapons. In the words of Governor John Winthrop, "We thought it better to trust God with our safety than to save ourselves by unrighteousness."⁸ Granted that the Puritan attitude was not flawless, we must admit that a sense of godly justice governed them. This is all the more notable given the fact that the settlers could be attacked by Indians at any time.

One interesting fact about the Indians is that most contemporary "Indians" are not even aware of their race. Our forefathers, far from wiping them out, mated with them; Indians married into English families. The simple reason the population on Indian reservations today is so small is that the majority of Indians have given up their identity and joined mainstream America. As an example, take the Cherokee Indians, whose mistreatment under Andrew Jackson was clearly evil. In 1751, this tribe numbered two thousand. On one recent occasion, when the tribe sued the United States government, the population was said to be fifty thousand. But the most interesting statistic, given to us by Greenway, is that 40 to 50 million Americans are proud to be one sixty-fourth Cherokee.⁹ Consider this fact: if 40 million Americans have one Cherokee ancestor six generations removed, even allowing for large families, this means a sizable number of Cherokee married settlers.

Despite the Puritan distrust of the Indians, the Puritans were still determined to be godly toward them. As Christians, the Puritans were anxious to convert the Indians to their faith. On a practical level, the Puritans were trying to save the Indians' souls from eternal damnation. Instead of being racist or considering the Indians as less than human, the Puritans came to realize that Indians were simply men without God; they were unconverted, still in a state of sin.[10] It was part of the legal duty of the county courts to "take care that the Indians residing in the severall sheires shal be civilized...and instructed in the knowledge & worship of god."[11] The Puritans knew the Indians had a primitive life-style, often immoral, sometimes bloody. They also knew that the only way the Indians would become civilized was through the power of the Christian Gospel.

Of all the missionaries to the Indians, the most famous was John Eliot, a man with a real concern for the Indians. One of his efforts was the translation of the Bible into the Indian tongue. His preaching was effective, resulting in the conversion of a large number of natives. One Puritan was moved to observe that upon arriving in New England "there was scarce any man that could believe that English grains would grow, or that the Plow could do any good...till experience taught them otherwise. So wee have thought of our Indian people, and therefore have beene discouraged to put plow to such dry and rocky ground." He said that his hope for Eliot's work was that it would show that "they are better soile for the Gospel than wee can thinke."[12]

These converted "praying Indians" sought to leave their wild way of life and live together in Christian villages governed by biblical law. They asked John Eliot for help. Eliot writes, "[the Indians] desired to leave their wild and scattered manner of life, and come under Civil Government and Order; which did put me upon search, after the mind of the Lord in that respect. And this VOW I did solemnly make unto the Lord concerning them; that they being a people without any forme of Government, and now to chuse; I would endeavour with all my might, to bring them under the Government of the Lord only. Namely that I would instruct them to embrace such Government, both Civil and Ecclesiastical, as the Lord hath commanded in the holy Scriptures and to deduce all their laws from the holy Scriptures, that so they may be the Lords people, ruled by him alone in all things. Which accordingly they have begun to do...."[13] These Indians formed slightly more than fourteen villages in New England and had a population of about thirty-six hundred.[14] A second edition of the Indian Old Testament had to be published because of demand. This edition was revised by Eliot, with assistance.[15] Why was the Old Testament more in demand than the New? A reasonable answer seems to be that, as God's instruction for civil law is found mainly in the Old Testament, the books were needed by the Indians as textbooks for their law.

The crowning act of forgiveness took place at the end of the terrible King Philip's War. After the Indians had finally been defeated, the Massachusetts victors could easily have killed those who survived. Instead of a bloody revenge, the Puritans provided the Indians with schools and missionaries.[16]

The Law

One of the most important things to remember about the law in all the colonies is that the British Parliament had no right to govern the colonists at all. The British Parliament's function was to make laws for Great Britain and nowhere else. The colonies were *Crown* colonies set by *royal* charters. This meant that the head of state in each colony was the king. Each colony had its own general assembly, which played the role that Parliament played in Britain. The situation was somewhat comparable to the British Commonwealth today. The Queen of England is also the Queen of New Zealand, Australia, Canada, and a host of other Commonwealth countries. Each of these countries shares the same head of state but has its own Parliament. Therefore, while the Queen of England has ceremonial authority in New Zealand, the British Parliament has none. As regards the American colonies, the only provision in their charters which restricted them was the one which prohibited them from passing any law contrary to the law of England. This principle of independence from Parliament would later be a vital issue in the American Revolution.

Parliament would, however, try from time to time to pass laws for the colonies. These attempts were resisted strongly. In 1678, the Massachusetts General Court (legislature) resisted an act of Parliament on navigation and trade. It stated: "Wee humbly conceive, according to the usuall sayings of the learned in the lawe, that the lawes of England are bounded within the fower seas, and doe not reach America...."[17]

Another interesting point to remember is that each colony had its own laws. There was no central government in America. Each colony was, in effect, a foreign country. Each colony had its own legislature, its own laws, and sometimes even minted its own money. Jefferson, writing in Virginia, once referred to the law of Massachusetts (along with the laws of Bermuda and Barbados) as "foreign law."[18]

Unless we keep these two facts in mind, it will be impossible to understand how the colonies were governed and why they broke with England in the 1770s.

Colonial law, especially in New England, was greatly influenced by the Bible. One striking example of this is found in the Body of Liberties of Massachusetts. In this set of laws, every capital crime (crime punishable by death) had the relevant Bible references attached for support.[19]

A few examples may prove interesting. The law stating that a stubborn or rebellious, incorrigible son be put to death came directly from the Bible.[20] Deuteronomy 21:18-21 NKJV states:

> If a man has a stubborn and rebellious son who will not obey the voice of his father or the voice of his mother, and who, when they have chastened him, will not heed them, then his father and his mother shall...bring him out to the elders of his city. And they shall say to the elders of his city, "This son of ours is stubborn and rebellious; he will not obey our voice; he is a glutton and a drunkard." Then all the men of his city shall stone him to death with stones; so you shall put away the evil person from among you....

Theft was another crime dealt with in a biblical way. A thief was ordered to make restitution (pay back what was stolen) to his victim, sometimes double or triple the amount involved.[21] Compare this with Exodus 22:1 and 4 NKJV: "If a man steals an ox or a sheep, and slaughters it or sells it, he shall restore five oxen for an ox and four sheep for a sheep....If the theft is certainly found alive in his hand, whether it is an ox or donkey or sheep, he shall restore double."

On the other hand, some colonial laws based on the Bible reflected its mercy rather than severity. For example, no criminal could be given more than forty strokes of the whip.[22] This agrees with Deuteronomy 25:3 NKJV: "Forty blows he may give him and no more, lest he should exceed this and beat him with many blows above these, and your brother be humiliated in your sight."

Finally, there is an interesting case of a bond servant who ran away from his master, William Drummond of Virginia, and fled to Massachusetts. A court in Boston released him from his service to Drummond, apparently on the authority of Deuteronomy 23:15: "You shall not give back to his master the slave who has escaped from his master to you" (NKJV). It ought to be pointed out that the governments of Virginia and Massachusetts argued about this case. Ultimately, Massachusetts made some of its citizens then in Virginia give £40 compensation to that colony. While Massachusetts was obviously of two minds on this case, what the Bible said clearly played a major role in court.[23]

It would be wrong to claim that biblical law was imposed at every point. Its main influence was felt in capital cases. As regards the rest of the law, it would be more accurate to say that the Bible had the power of the veto; that is to say, no laws would be established that went against the Bible, although not all of them actually were found there.[24]

This brings us to an important question: In Puritan New England, was there a separation of Church and State? The answer is that the government was not ruled by the Church; it was, however, obedient to the Bible. The Bible gives instruction on how Church and State are to conduct themselves. Neither of them has absolute control over the other. God, through the Bible, rules them both. Separation of Church and State gives both freedom from each other, *not freedom from God.*

It is possible to see separation of Church and State in the history of Puritan Massachusetts. For instance, the 1629 royal charter did not give any special privileges to the Church. The charter did not have any ministers among the men to whom it was granted. Furthermore, ministers never sought to hold public office or to run the government. They might seek to advise the State, but never to control it.

Puritan law treated all men equally. Church members were dealt with the same way as anyone else. On the other hand, a church had the right to discipline any of its members even if they were officers of the government. However, the only punishments the Church could impose were religious ones such as excommunication, restriction from the sacraments, etc. A man could not be removed from public office by the Church.

On the other hand, churches were allowed to operate as they saw fit, within certain restrictions. For instance, from 1659 to 1681, it was forbidden by law to celebrate Christmas, because it was believed that the observances had become pagan.[25]

The principles governing Church and State were set forth in the Body of Liberties as follows:

58. Civill Authoritie hath power and libertie to see the peace, ordinances and Rules of Christ observed in every church according to his word. So it be done in a Civill and not in an Ecclesiastical way.
59. Civill Authoritie hath power and libertie to deale with any Church member in a way of Civill Justice, notwithstanding any Church relation, office or interest.
60. No church censure shall degrad or depose any man from any Civill dignitie, office, or Authoritie he shall have in the Commonwealth.[26]

We must note here that Massachusetts law had a great influence far outside its time or place. The Body of Liberties had a great influence on the Founding Fathers of the United States. When Massachusetts adopted the Body of Liberties, it made clear that it was held to be desirable to place important principles of law into writing. Therefore, a written constitution for America was given inspiration; this resulted in first, the Articles of Confederation and then, the United States Constitution as we have it today. This was a break in tradition from Great Britain. The British constitution was, and is, an unwritten one based upon tradition and the precedents of court rulings on constitutional questions.[27]

The particular laws of Massachusetts, as they were developed through experience and trial and error, also had an influence on the other colonies. These colonies recognized the importance of the Massachusetts experience. Sharing as they did the same faith in God, they were quite willing to take parts of the Massachusetts statutes and put them into their own legal systems.[28]

It is also important to notice that Puritan New England had a government limited by the law in what it could do. The leaders of the colonies recognized this; they never felt that they, or the State, were above the law, but always beneath it.[29]

It is a pleasure to learn that, unlike popular myth, there was a good deal of grace in Puritan law. There was no reign of terror in the Puritan colonies.

The saying "Ignorance of the law is no excuse" did not always hold true in Massachusetts. As there were no mass media to make the law known, if a court was convinced that the citizen accused of a crime was ignorant of the law, it would be inclined to be lenient, or even find the person innocent.

Those found guilty of capital crimes were not always put to death. Various factors, such as his standing in the community and the evidence of repentance, would be considered in the punishment of the guilty party. Governor Winthrop had justified this practice from Scripture, pointing out that there were those who were not put to death for crimes which the law of Moses said were capital. Neither King David nor Bathsheba were put to death for adultery, for example.[30]

There were other ways in which Massachusetts law was less strict than English law. Puritan divorce laws were more liberal, especially in the rights given to the wife. Laws dealing with the inheritance of land by aliens were easier as well. In criminal trials, the Puritans granted the accused the right of bail and the right to appeal against their conviction. Neither of these liberties was automatically guaranteed in Great Britain.[31]

The Puritans were not a vindictive people. They were concerned with much more than merely seeing that each criminal paid for his crimes. They were also concerned that the soul of the criminal might be made right with God and his behavior corrected. Toward this goal, efforts would be made to encourage a criminal to mend his ways and reform.[32]

The Holy Commonwealth

Why were the Puritans so careful to have laws that did not violate the teaching of the Bible? Why was the church the center of village life in New England? The reason was that Puritans saw Christians as a religious family. They did not migrate to America to establish a community with many points of view, all tolerated. They were a spiritual family, transplanted to America as a group, in order to set up a society whose leader was God and whose law book was primarily the Bible.

The Puritans were not Yankee individualists, that later rugged breed that was proudly self-sufficient, neither needing nor wanting the interest and advice of others. On the other hand, the Puritans were not socialists setting up a commune where the all-wise State, pretending to be God, made all their decisions for them.

They were something special. They were a family of those who were born-again Christians. They were a group of people who thought the same way, God's way. Gathered together, they desired to set up a community in New England that was uniquely Christian. They wanted to take the wilderness and subdue it, tame it for Jesus Christ. They took seriously God's command to Adam which had never been withdrawn: "Be fruitful and multiply; fill the earth and subdue it; have dominion over the fish of the sea, over the birds of the air, and over every living thing that moves on the earth."[33] There is a world of difference between *subduing* the earth, which was what the Puritans worked to do, and *killing* the earth, which is what certain thoughtless individuals are doing.

As in politics there were various schools of thought, generally grouped into political parties, so the same is to be found in all Christian faiths. The Puritans, in common with nearly all American Christians up to the mid 1700s, were of the way of thinking called Calvinism. John Calvin, after whom Calvinism is named, was a Protestant leader of the Reformation and perhaps the greatest Christian philosopher in the Church since Saint Augustine. His emphasis, put in extremely simple terms, was that God is King of all creation. Calvinists generally consider God as King in two ways: first, He created everything, and He decided what was going to happen to every little part of His creation. Nothing was left out of His plan. Most important, God decided who was going to be saved (these are the ones for whom Jesus died); every event that would happen to every living creature is also under God's management; God also planned every event that would happen to the world of matter around us—the stars, the weather, the trees, earthquakes, everything.

Second, Calvinism holds that, since God created mankind, He is the only one with the right to tell us how to live, to let us know what is good and what is bad. As people created by God, we have the duty to keep God's Law as found in the Bible. The punishment for failure is death in hell. Since we have all failed, we deserve to go to hell. Salvation is all of grace. God sent His Son to die for those He chose to forgive. Jesus took the punishment. The fact that we cannot keep God's Law perfectly does not excuse us from the duty to seek to keep it.

Calvin also had strong views about the world: Christians were to band together. If, working as a team, they labored hard and were careful in their affairs, they could subdue the world for God. With His help, they could take over the world of art, the world of government, the world of science; they could exercise dominion. Calvinism fathered a work ethic toward this goal—God's kingdom on earth.

Even when New Englanders began to drift in their doctrine, they still retained the Calvinist emphasis on work and dominion. They held to this, making it a part of the American character, even while, unfortunately, abandoning the religious side of Calvinism. This is why a historian could accurately refer to "Calvinist Catholics," although religious Calvinism has been anti-Catholic. The Calvinistic view of the world is possible without the theology. In modern times it is sometimes called "the Protestant work ethic." In the beginning, Puritans were religious Calvinists; in time, their heirs became less religious, but they retained the Calvinistic desire for freedom, community, and hard work. Our America is the result.

Because the Puritans believed the community should remain closely knit, they were not happy about those who wished to move out into the unsettled land beyond the settlements. Some ministers said that for men to move to isolated places away from the churches was to submit to the temptations of the wilderness. One of their leading ministers, John Cotton, urged the people never to settle anywhere without good ministers. He even suggested that a law be passed stating that "noe man shall set his dwelling house" more than "half a myle at the farthest, from the meeting house of the congregation."[34] In fact, the colonial authorities made the settlers at the plantation of Nashaway abandon their settlement because they could not support a minister there.[35] The Puritans were keenly aware that uncontrolled expansion without spiritual supervision would lead to the weakening of religious influence and a loosening of the ties of the spiritual community.

The Puritans' attitude toward expanding into the wilderness had its contradictions. On the one hand, they believed they had a mission to tame the wilderness and to exercise dominion over it in the name of Christ. On the other hand, they discouraged pioneers from moving too far from the settlements because of the importance they placed on having a strong spiritual community, the Holy Commonwealth.[36] There was, however, no stopping the spirit of exploration in the colony. Men went out seeking new land to explore, and to settle new pioneer villages. In this movement away from the established communities, the Puritans saw the beginning of the end of the Holy Commonwealth.

The truth of the matter was that other causes were at work, too, bringing down the high level of religion. To find these causes, one need not venture outside the Puritan strongholds.

As the economic situation improved in New England, the settlers felt less need to trust the Lord for their daily bread. The sense of desperation and dependence was gone. Things were getting more comfortable, although in many ways this proved to be a false sense of security. Nevertheless, as long as the colonists were feeling confortable and content, they were less likely to feel any need for God.

Added to the improved standard of living was the fact that the makeup of the population was changing. Reports of the good life had reached Europe, and boatloads, seeking their fame and fortune, were arriving all the time. The population of the colonies increased rapidly. The days of scattered hamlets of a dozen or so families were over. In all the colonies, cities such as Boston, Philadelphia, and New York were growing rapidly. While in itself there was no harm in this growth, it was, however, a different group of people, with different motives for emigrating than the early Puritans, who had come to set up the kingdom of God in New England. The new immigrants were more materialistic and self-centered. While these people still considered themselves religious and went to church, the devotion to God demonstrated by the first settlers was not there.

The leadership of the colony was also changing. With the passing of time, the first leaders of the colony died. In their places a new type of ruling class developed. As the colony began to produce goods to export back to England, the merchants of the colony began to prosper and gain influence. While these leaders were regular in their attendance at church, they had an eye to business which influenced them more than their dedication to Christ. As priorities changed, so slowly as to be hardly noticed, the idea of a spiritual community, a church family, or a Holy Commonwealth faded.[37]

One indication of this change can be found in the changing attitudes of the ministers. Samuel Willard, giving the 1690 election sermon, commented, "A People are not made for Rulers, But Rulers for a People."[38] The original Puritans would not have agreed with this. They would have said that laws should be based on God's law. God gave us His Law so that we might conduct our affairs according to His will. Rulers, however chosen, were the servants of God to maintain an orderly and godly way of life. These newer ideas were man-centered, whereas before society had been God-centered. In embryo form these were the same ideas now behind our modern humanist governments.

As religious life became more formal and traditional in the closing years of the seventeenth century, the old-line Puritans struck back. As a way of warning the people, they began to preach what today we call "hell-fire preaching." This sort of preaching is commonly believed to be a typical Puritan emphasis, revealing a holy delight in the sufferings of the damned. This was not the case. The earlier years of New England saw no Puritan emphasis on hell-fire. Such preaching was only resorted to when it was felt that the time had come to sound a spiritual warning.[39] It was motivated by a concern for loved ones and friends who were strangers to Christ.

Another defensive action was taken by the Puritans to guard the religious purity of the churches. Up until this time, the Puritans' Congregational churches had been free to run their own affairs and to choose their own ministers. However, these churches were beginning to select men who were willing to compromise and tone down their sermons to give men an easy Gospel. The Puritans persuaded the colonial governments to alter the government of the churches. Henceforth, a central control would seek to ensure that the churches and ministers were kept in line. Connecticut established the Saybrook Platform in 1708, virtually turning the independent Congregational churches into a centrally organized Presbyterian denomination. In 1705, its neighboring colony had adopted the Massachusetts Proposals, which were designed to do the same thing.[40]

Although the Puritans took actions to protect their own churches, they realized that there was growing disunity in the Holy Commonwealth. Various other Protestant denominations had arisen with no desire to worship with the rest of the Christian family in the town church. In the more casual spiritual conditions of the day, it was no longer possible to keep the unity of the Christian community by forbidding people to worship on their own. Indeed, this would now cause more problems than it would solve. Even the great preaching family, the Mathers, were ready not only for toleration but even fellowship with the dissenters.[41]

Connecticut passed its Toleration Act in 1708, in the same year it passed the Saybrook Platform, and by this act allowed dissenting Protestants to worship in their own churches, although they still had to pay the religious tax to support the local established minister. This tax money continued to be paid to the town church until 1727, when the Anglicans were allowed to have their religious taxes diverted to the support of their own minister. This same right was given to the Quakers and the Baptists in 1729. Toleration came to Massachusetts by a slightly different route. The new charter, reflecting the new spirit of toleration in England, did away with the religious qualifications required in order to be allowed to vote. After receiving this charter, it was only a matter of time until Massachusetts, too, allowed religious tax money to be given to dissenting ministers. For the Anglicans, this came about in 1727. The Quakers got the same right in 1731, as did the Baptists in 1735. Everyone knew that toleration was here to stay when the Mathers, pillars of the Establishment, assisted in the ordination of a Baptist minister.[42] The older ideal of the Holy Commonwealth was finished.

The Great Awakening

The place was Northhampton, Massachusetts; the time was December 1734. The event was the start of a work by the Holy Spirit soon to shake the colonies to the roots of their religious foundations.

At this time, Jonathan Edwards had been pastor of the Northhampton church for five years. Edwards had first come to Northhampton in 1727, at the age of twenty-four, to be assistant minister to his aged grandfather, Samuel Stoddard. Two years later Pastor Stoddard died, and Edwards became the church's minister. One looks in vain for anything special about this man. It could be said that he was prepared to speak his mind fearlessly, but that alone could not explain what was to come.

But come it did. In the latter half of December 1734, the people of Northhampton began to feel anxious about their relationship with God. In that month alone five or six people gave evidence of having been converted. Edwards was particularly surprised by the visit of a young woman well known for her loose moral behavior. To his shock, she had changed. Her way of life had become more holy; she had a serious concern to become right with God. Out of the blue, seemingly, she had been converted. She was not the only one.

One Sunday in the spring of 1735, Edwards received one hundred new members into his church, all of whom showed evidence of having been born again. The town was transformed. In the words of Edwards:

"...the town seemed to be full of the presence of God. It never was so full of love, nor so full of joy...there were remarkable tokens of God's presence in almost every house. It was a time of joy....Our public assemblies were then beautiful; the congregation was alive in God's service, everyone earnestly intent on the public worship, every hearer eager to drink the words of the minister as they came from his mouth. The assembly in general were, from time to time, in tears while the word was preached, some weeping with sorrow and distress, others with joy and love, others with pity and concern for their neighbors."[43]

And it spread. From town to town in New England the Spirit moved, giving yet more people a like experience of the grace of God. Nor did it stop there. Similar experiences of a Great Awakening were taking place in the middle colonies as well. The Holy Spirit, after a period of religious deadness, was on the move.

The leaders of this movement were all Calvinists in their religious views, but the revival had brought in a different perspective. Neither were they like some revivalists of our time who, in their extreme form, seem to believe in salvation by the simple act of raising one's hand or walking to the front during an evangelistic meeting.

George Whitefield, a gifted English evangelist and the greatest British preacher for decades, had no equal until C. H. Spurgeon of the next century. Whitefield, a Calvinistic Methodist, spent much of his time in America, where he died in 1770. During 1739 and 1740, Whitefield toured the colonies. His expressive style and moving speech made him a popular preacher. Even Benjamin Franklin of Philadelphia was impressed by this young man and became his firm friend.[44]

At the same time, though, the wind of the Spirit was blowing in New Jersey. The Lord used the Dutch preacher the Reverend Theodore J. Frelinghuysen to spark off an awakening to the Gospel. One man profoundly influenced by Frelinghuysen was the Reverend Gilbert Tennent, who became one of the leaders of the Great Awakening. Tennent's style was more of the roaring, stamping nature than Whitefield's, but the Lord used him, too.[45]

From the beginning, the Great Awakening was highly emotional, increasingly so as time went on. This brought great opposition from the established denominations. New Jersey, home of Frelinghuysen and Tennent, was a good example of this. The Presbyterian Church in that colony went through the agony of sharp difference of opinion over what was happening. Those who favored the status quo and distrusted the upsurge in religious emotions were called the "Old Side"; those who welcomed this new interest in the Gospel which was sweeping many into the Church were called the "New Side." So bitter did the split become that in 1741 the denomination broke in two. The New Side with its expansionism soon grew larger as the conservative Old Side, trying to prevent any change from religion as they knew it, became smaller. Eventually, in 1758, they reunited; perhaps it would be more accurate to say that the minority Old Side gave in and joined the New Side.[46]

The reaction of the established churches against the Great Awakening was caused, in great part, by the emotional scenes which took place at their gatherings. In almost every movement some hangers-on will exploit the excitement and attention. By their strange behavior, these eccentrics often bring a bad reputation to all concerned. So it was with the Great Awakening. Certainly there was strong emotion as sinners repented of their sins and came to conversion under the preaching of great men such as Tennent, Whitefield, Edwards, and others. There was nothing wrong with this, nor is there any record of moral sin connected with it. It was the lunatic fringe which caused unholy bedlam. It was this group, exploiting the Great Awakening, which came close to discrediting the entire movement.

Another force attacking the Great Awakening was the rationalistic Arminians. Historian William G. McLoughlin has described eighteenth-century Arminianism thus:

> To be an Arminian in the language of the Separates was not so much to preach the theological heresies of Arminius [the revivalists themselves came close to Arminianism in practice if not theology, while John Wesley, Whitefield's mentor, did in fact espouse Arminianism in 1740]. The most obvious aspect of what the pietists of the Awakening meant by Arminianism was a kind of "formality," spiritual dullness, preaching the letter of the gospel without its spirit, with "the Spirit." This meant the pervasive use of logic, theological exposition, or sophisticated doctrinal argument to appeal to the reason or understanding of lost sinners. Arminian preachers seemed to consider man a rational being whose will could be moved by appeals to reason.[48]

The Arminian belief of that period was that leading a life obedient to the commands of the Bible was important for salvation. If a man by his own free will obeyed God, then it was clear he was God's child. If he chose to disobey God, he was either not saved in the first place or had lost his salvation. These rationalistic Arminians disliked the Calvinists' teaching that salvation, being paid for by Jesus' death on the cross, meant that one could become a Christian without justifying works. Added to seeing the emotional extremes of the fringe, it appeared to them that those in the Great Awakening wanted a loss of all self-control as a mark of being a Christian.

Those within the Great Awakening attacked these Arminians as being traditional, formal Christians. They accused them of being more interested in outwardly following rules than in seeking to have God's free grace in their hearts. The Calvinists of the Awakening held that if Jesus paid for the sins of those who would be saved by His death on the cross, there was no further price for salvation to be paid by the sinner; to insist that the sinner needed to add something was an insult to the cross of Christ.

We must point out that the battle lines between religious Calvinists and Arminians have shifted somewhat since the 1700s. It is important to remember, when reading about the Calvinist-Arminian controversy of the eighteenth century, that we cannot identify everything they stood for then with their spiritual descendants of the twentieth century.

In Virginia, where the Anglican Church was the denomination established by the government, feelings ran high. The Anglican Church had a large element of Scottish and Irish Presbyterians in it. This group was divided for and against Whitefield and the Awakening. They did, however, take advantage of the climate of religious civil war to rebel against the Anglican authority's imposition upon the local churches. The result of this rebellion was victory. The law was changed, giving the churches the right to choose their own ministers (they had done this in the past, but now it was official).[49]

In New England, the controversy became intense. The Congregationalists were split into two groups, the "Old Lights" and the "New Lights." Their points of view were similar to those of the Old Side and New Side in New Jersey. The New Lights, not approving of the "dead" ministry of the parish ministers, split away and formed their own separate Congregational churches.

The Connecticut government overreacted badly. In 1742, a law was passed which denied permission for anyone to preach in a parish without the invitation of the established minister there. The next year the colony repealed the Toleration Act. The legislature assumed the power of permitting dissenting congregations of other denominations (for example, Baptists and Quakers) to worship. The New Lights, organized as separate Congregational churches, did not gain this permission. The legislature said that they were not a true denomination like the Baptists, but simply troublemakers within the Congregational Church. These actions did not make the New Lights any more friendly toward the Old Lights. The New Lights fought back politically. In 1750, persecution of the New Lights ceased. In 1758, the New Lights were strong enough to win an election and form the government of Connecticut.[50] Earlier, the Puritans had wanted to build a society, a community with God as King. That dream had died as men lost their fervent interest in the faith. Here at last was a dramatic new religious movement; with all these new Christians, surely the idea of a truly Christian society could be recovered! But it was not to be. The new emphasis was on seeing individuals converted, a vital first step, but with little vision beyond that. Meanwhile, the colonial governments, through sinful actions, had plunged America into an economic crisis. The Great Awakening, taking hold of the Puritans' dream, could have radically changed things. However, as Hildreth bluntly put it, "They made it their prominent idea not so much to save the commonwealth as to save themselves."[51] Both issues should have had their concern.

Not all shared this retreat from the world. George Whitefield saw the need for the Church to concern itself with the social problems of the day. One of his projects was to set up an orphanage in Georgia. As he went around preaching, he not only looked for conversion but also for contributions; he took up offerings which were sent to his Georgia orphanage.[52]

Politically, the New Lights of Connecticut would have taught their fellow followers of the Great Awakening. If the Connecticut government was going to persecute this group of Christians, then it was high time for these Christians to take over the government. And so they did. The New Lights soon became a commanding force in Connecticut. Bushman wrote, "In 1763, William Johnson marveled that the New Lights who in his memory 'were a small party, merely a religious one,' had 'acquired such an influence as to be nearly the ruling part of the government owing to their superior attention to civil affairs and close union among themselves in politics.' "⁵³

Economics

Just before and during the Great Awakening, the economic situation in the colonies was becoming serious. In December 1690, Massachusetts was in debt. In order to liquidate its obligations, the colony printed £7,000 worth of paper money. The colony promised that in a year's time it would pay a pound's worth of silver or gold (the normal currency at that time) for every paper pound printed. Although technically this might be called a loan, those slips of paper credit were meant to be used as money. The colony also promised not to issue any more such "money" in the future. It broke both promises. In just one year, the money that had been printed lost 40 percent of its value. If you find it easier to think of prices rising rather than the value of money falling (which amounts to the same thing) you could say that Massachusetts had an annual inflation rate of 66.6 percent.⁵⁴ Printing money makes its value depreciate. Simply put, the more there is of something, the less it is worth, and paper money is artificial money; its value is typographical, not real. Money made out of paper is the easiest thing in the world to print. Massachusetts needed some money to pay its debts, and so it printed some. Good money which maintains its value is generally made from either gold or silver. It is much harder to find more gold and silver to make coins with than it is to get some paper and ink! With gold and silver coinage the government cannot flood the market with paper money, destroying its value. Because the amount of gold and silver in the world is limited, this means that the metal has a certain value to it which no government can destroy. The Massachusetts government, having printed its money, then said that this money had to be treated exactly as the old silver coins were. This is the brutality of what is called a "legal tender" law. Shopkeepers had to accept payment of accounts in increasingly depreciating paper. Put bluntly, Massachusetts Colony made everyone poorer in order to get itself out of debt. Like all inflation, it was theft.

In Massachusetts, the printing of paper money increased. In 1690, Massachusetts had £200,000 in silver circulating in the colony. By 1714, there was £240,000 of money in Massachusetts, but it was all paper. In 1714, the official price of silver was 7 shillings to the ounce (there were 20 shillings to the pound). However, the price one would have to pay on the open market was 9 shillings in paper money; that's an increase of over 28 percent.[56] With paper money, gold and silver appreciate in value as the paper depreciates.

Almost all the colonies got into the paper-money business. It was particularly attractive to buy things from England in British pounds (based on silver), then pay for these goods in the cheaper colonial currencies. At one point the Crown told South Carolina to print no more money. The colony evaded that problem by making rice legal tender.[56]

The same story was repeated elsewhere. In 1739, Pennsylvania had £80,000 circulating in the colony, but it was only worth £50,000 in silver. The money in Massachusetts continued to grow. There was £300,000 in 1744, £1,500,000 in 1746, and £2,500,000 in 1748. Comparing money to silver, the price rose from 6 shillings an ounce in 1700 to 60 shillings an ounce in 1748, a price increase of 900 percent. All the paper money lost value so rapidly that a 1750 pound in Connecticut was worth just one-ninth of a 1700 pound; a pound from the Carolinas was one-tenth the value as in 1700; Massachusetts was one-eleventh and Rhode Island a whopping one twenty-third.[57]

All the paper money issues promised to pay the owner back at a later date with real money, usually silver. As the amounts printed increased, the promises became more and more of a joke. The economy was rescued after King George's War, when Britain paid the colonies an indemnity payment in hard British cash. The colonies used this money to redeem the paper and to put its currencies back on a solid footing. Parliament prohibited the colonies from printing any more. Except for that payment, the colonies would have been over the brink into economic disaster.[58]

Printing worthless money was not the only economic sin during this period. Trying to avoid paying debts, especially British ones, was a popular pastime. In 1708, Maryland passed a law allowing a man to declare bankruptcy to avoid paying his debts. The Crown vetoed that law. Parliament went further and, in 1732, said a man's land and slaves could be taken to pay off his debts.[59]

Another important economic activity was slavery. Slavery was a way of receiving labor without having to pay for it in wages. Slavery was legal throughout the colonies and, contrary to popular belief, the northern colonies were as guilty as the southern ones. For instance, Boston in the 1750s had a greater proportion of slaves in its population than did Baltimore before the Civil War. Another startling fact is that colonial New York City had a population which was one-sixth slaves. Its slavery laws were as harsh as those in Virginia.[60]

Furthermore, the slave trade was vital to the economy of New England. Those colonies were not allowed to export wheat and salted food to Britain. Therefore, New England merchants had to earn their income another way. They did this by sailing to Africa and buying slaves. These slaves were taken to the West Indies, where they were exchanged for molasses and sugar, which were shipped back to New England to be made into rum. This rum was then shipped to Africa to pay for the slaves. In the matter of the slave trade, no area of America comes away without guilt.[61]

Having established the fact that the entire colonial American society was involved with slavery, we must add that the slaves were not treated as badly as we are led to believe. In Massachusetts, slaves were given the same rights as apprentices. Slavery was morally wrong, but so is misrepresentation. Another law permitted a master to free any of his slaves, but not without giving security to the parish that the freed man would not become a burden on the locality.[62] Provision had to be made for him. This fact was ignored by the abolitionists of the middle nineteenth century.

The South had laws protecting the slaves as well. In the colony of Georgia, slaves could not be worked on Sunday subject to a fine of £5. The slaves also had to attend church. Furthermore, they could not be worked more than fourteen hours in the winter and fifteen in the summer. This law was also enforced by a fine of £5. A master who did not provide food, clothes, and shelter for his slaves was also fined.[63]

There was another kind of slavery as well, the economic slavery which Britain imposed on the colonies. Britain never intended that the colonies should have healthy, independent economies. Their function was to provide Britain with raw materials and a market for their goods. In other words, the colonies were there to be used for the benefit of Great Britain. This policy which prohibited the colonies from trading with other countries was called mercantilism.[64] The first mercantile laws were passed in 1650 and 1651, and banned all exports of colonial products to England in ships that were not owned or manned by the English. Also, other European countries were not allowed to send goods to the colonies unless they came in English ships. Further, goods for the colonies were banned that came from nations other than the one in which the merchandise was produced. The screw was tightened further with the Navigation Act of 1660. This act banned all non-English or American ships with a crew less than 75 percent English. Also, the ships themselves had to have been built in Britain. The economy of the colonies was sent reeling with blow after blow from England. Another devastating regulation concerned the "enumerated articles." These were goods on a list which could be sold only from one colony to another or to England. This list included things such as sugar and tobacco.[65] Then the Staple Act of 1663 forbade any foreign imports into the colonies that did not pass through England—and have English duties paid on them. In 1705 and 1722 more goods were added to the enumerated-articles list. At this time also, the Navigation Act of 1696 allowed customs agents to enter private property without a search warrant in their search for smugglers.

Britain also tried to smother trade in colonial goods which it was felt formed a threat to British products. As New England's wool industry began to rival Britain's, the Wool Act of 1699 was passed. This act banned the export of finished or raw wool, not only to England but from one colony to another as well. Yankee ingenuity got around that law by simply herding the sheep across the colonial borders before shearing the wool!

Some of the restrictions were especially totalitarian. The Hat Act of 1732 is a case in point. This act included the law prohibiting the importation of hats from one colony to another. Also, hats could only be made by men who had served seven years as apprentices, and there were precious few of them, as each firm was limited to two, neither of which could be a Negro.

The only good thing about those mercantile laws was that for the first fifty years of the eighteenth century they were not enforced. Edmund Burke, America's great friend in Britain's House of Commons, called this lack of law enforcement "salutary neglect."

Whig Prime Minister Walpole, in power during a good deal of this period, was more respectful of the colonies than was the Tory party. He was once asked about the idea of taxing the colonies in order to benefit England. He replied, "I will leave that for some man bolder than I am, and less a friend of British commerce."[66] The prime ministers who were to follow him did not turn out to be bolder, and by no means as wise.

During all this time, a dangerous development was under way. Earlier, the Bible had been seen as God's Word for all of life, for family,

Church, State, business, and school. Now, slowly, the Bible was becoming a church book, and the world was moving toward "freedom" from God, a characteristic which identifies us in the twentieth century.

Chapter 4 Notes

1. Peter N. Carroll, *Puritanism and the Wilderness* (New York: Columbia University Press, 1969), pp. 10–11, 76–77.
2. Ibid., pp. 79, 169–170.
3. John Greenway, *The American Tradition—a Gallery of Rogues* (New York: Mason/Charter, 1977), pp. 19, 21.
4. Ibid., p. 20.
5. Ibid., pp. 5–6.
6. Edwin Powers, *Crime and Punishment in Early Massachusetts 1620–1692* (Boston: Beacon Press, 1966), p. 44.
7. Ibid., p. 210.
8. Carroll, *Puritanism*, pp. 92–93.
9. Greenway, *American Tradition*, pp. 18–19.
10. Carroll, *Puritanism*, pp. 11–12.
11. Massachusetts Colonial Records (1644) as quoted in Powers, *Crime and Punishment*, p. 61.
12. Carroll, *Puritanism*, pp. 123–124.
13. John Eliot, *The Christian Commonwealth* (New York: Arno Press, 1659, reprinted 1972), ninth page of unnumbered introduction.
14. Richard Hildreth, *The History of the United States of America* (New York: Harper & Brothers, 1881), vol. 1, p. 479.
15. Ibid., vol. 1, p. 493.
16. Carroll, *Puritanism*, pp. 214–215.
17. Massachusetts Colonial Records (1678) as quoted in Powers, *Crime and Punishment*, p. 85.
18. George Lee Haskins, *Law and Authority in Early Massachusetts* (New York: Macmillan, 1960), pp. 6–7.
19. Richard L. Perry, ed., *Sources of Our Liberties* (Chicago: American Bar Foundation, 1959), pp. 158–159.
20. Powers, *Crime and Punishment*, pp. 268–269.
21. Ibid., p. 410.
22. Ibid., p. 92.

23. Hildreth, *History of the United States*, vol. 1, p. 92.
24. Haskins, *Law and Authority*, pp. 130–131.
25. Powers, *Crime and Punishment*, pp. 107–108.
26. Perry, *Sources*, p. 154.
27. Haskins, *Law and Authority*, p. 231.
28. Ibid., p. 221.
29. Ibid., p. 56.
30. Powers, *Crime and Punishment*, pp. 77, 274–287.
31. Haskins, *Law and Authority*, pp. 195, 198–199.
32. Ibid., pp. 211–212.
33. *The New King James Bible* (Nashville: Thomas Nelson Publishers, 1982), Genesis 1:28.
34. Carroll, *Puritanism*, p. 121.
35. Ibid., p. 122.
36. Ibid., pp. 220–222.
37. Chard Powers Smith, *Yankees and God* (New York: Hermitage House, 1954), pp. 188–190, 196.
38. Haskins, *Law and Authority*, pp. 229–230.
39. Smith, *Yankees*, pp. 202–203.
40. Murray N. Rothbard, *Conceived in Liberty* (New Rochelle, New York: Arlington House, 1975), vol. 2, pp. 23, 25.
41. William G. McLoughlin, *New England Dissent* (Cambridge: Harvard University Press, 1971), vol. 1, p. 334.
42. Smith, *Yankees*, pp. 230–233.
43. Peter Marshall and David Manuel, *The Light and the Glory* (Old Tappan, New Jersey: Fleming H. Revell Company, 1977), p. 242. See pp. 240–253 for a fuller account of the Great Awakening.
44. Smith, *Yankees*, p. 255; Rothbard, *Conceived*, vol. 2, pp. 160–161.
45. Smith, *Yankees*, pp. 255–256; Rothbard, *Conceived*, vol. 2, pp. 160–161.
46. Rothbard, *Conceived*, vol. 2, p. 163.
47. Smith, *Yankees*, p. 258.
48. McLoughlin, *Dissent*, vol. 1, pp. 350–351.
49. Hildreth, *History of the United States*, vol. 2, p. 338.
50. Smith, *Yankees*, pp. 258–259; McLoughlin, *Dissent*, vol. 1, p. 362; Rothbard, *Conceived*, vol. 2, pp. 162, 197.
51. Hildreth, *History of the United States*, vol. 2, pp. 390–391.
52. McLoughlin, *Dissent*, vol. 1, p. 386; Marshall and Manuel, *Light and the Glory*, p. 248.
53. Rousas John Rushdoony, *God's Plan for Victory* (Fairfax, Virginia: Thoburn Press, 1980), pp. 26–27.
54. Rothbard, *Conceived*, vol. 2, pp. 130–131.
55. Ibid., pp. 131–132.

56. Hildreth, *History of the United States*, vol. 2, p. 290.
57. Ibid., pp. 257–258; Rothbard, *Conceived*, vol. 2, p. 137; article "The Middle Colonies" by Berthold Fernow in Narrative and *Critical History of America*, edited by Justin Winsor (Boston: Houghton Mifflin, 1887), vol. 5, part 1, p. 213.
58. Rothbard, *Conceived*, vol. 2, p. 138.
59. Ibid., vol. 2, pp. 83–84.
60. Hildreth, *History of the United States*, vol. 2, p. 322.
61. Rothbard, *Conceived*, vol. 2, pp. 212–213.
62. Hildreth, *History of the United States*, vol. 2, p. 419.
63. Ibid., vol. 2, pp. 418, 422.
64. Unless otherwise noted, the information on mercantilism is from Rothbard, *Conceived*, vol. 2, pp. 202, 205–208.
65. In addition to Rothbard see Hildreth, *History of the United States*, vol. 1, p. 513.
66. Ibid., vol. 2, p. 322.

Religious Faith and
The American War for Independence

FIVE

"The second day of July, 1776," wrote John Adams, "will be the most memorable epoch in the history of America. I am apt to believe that it will be celebrated by succeeding generations as the great anniversary festival."[1] Adams was close. America seems to have that forward-looking character which, even back then, tempted men to speculate on the nation's future and to anticipate its greatness.

The whole story of the War for Independence is one of the most dramatic in the history of our continent. We all know the basic history of our country. We all know the basic history of that war to some extent. America fought for independence against the British and won. The reasons for the war are less known.

We discussed the first reason for the war in the last chapter: the interference of the British Parliament with the royal colonies. The colonists at first were angry with Parliament rather than the king. As Jefferson said:

The addition of new States to the British empire had produced an addition of new, and, sometimes opposite interests. It is now, therefore, the great office of his Majesty to resume the exercise of his negative power, and to prevent the passage of laws by any one legislature of the empire which might bear injuriously on the rights and interests of another.[2]

James Wilson, a signer of the Declaration of Independence, said in 1770, "All the different members of the British empire are distinct states, Independent of each other, but connected together under the same soverign."[3] This same thought was present in the American atti-

73

tude toward the position. One British officer was scornful when he learned that the Rebels referred to their army as the "king's troops" and to the British army as "Parliament's." Most Americans are unaware of this very important fact of history. Resistance against the government of Great Britain and war against the king were two different issues at the beginning of the war. The colonies were under the Crown, not Parliament, and Parliament's attempt to control them was seen as the attempt of a foreign power to supplant their civil governments.

The second reason for the colonists' resistance stems from the actions of Parliament. The Americans resisted the taxes laid down by that body upon the colonies. In the last chapter we saw how the colonies submitted to very tight restrictions upon their trade, rules and regulations as many as the sands of the sea. That was bad enough. For Parliament to go one step further and try to tax them was the last straw. This taxation had England's mercantilist benefits in mind and was hostile to America's interests.

On March 22, 1765, the British Parliament passed the Stamp Act. This was the first time that Parliament had tried to directly tax the American colonies. As a postage stamp shows that the postage money has been paid for the delivery of a letter, in the same way customs officials were to place a stamp on articles of trade to show that the duty had been paid.

This act caused a great protest. It was more than a matter of the American people protesting against the British people. Those sympathetic with the Tory party on both sides of the Atlantic approved of the act. Members of the Whig party in England were as much against the Parliament's colonial policies as were the Whigs in America.

In the face of massive colonial protest in America and disapproval at home, the following year Parliament repealed the act. However, around the same time this law was repealed, two other measures were passed. First, the Declaratory Act proclaimed Parliament's authority over the colonies "in all cases whatsoever."[4] Second, as if to drive the point home, Parliament passed a small, symbolic tax of three pence a pound on tea imported into the colony by English merchants.

This, of course, resulted in the Boston Tea Party. After the Massachusetts royal governor refused to allow the ship to leave port with its cargo still on board, the colonists decided it was better to destroy the tea rather than pay the tax. Taking care that no one stole any of the tea, it was dumped into the harbor.

This did destroy British property, but Parliament's reaction was out of proportion to the crime. The reason was Parliament knew that, while the crime was the destruction of some tea, it symbolized colonial contempt for Parliament's claimed authority. For this reason, Parliament closed the Port of Boston; this action did nothing to soothe colonial tempers.

Another very important reason for the War for Independence was based on religion. It concerns the efforts made to establish an Anglican bishop in the colonies. Like the tea, the establishment of a bishop was a symbol of Parliament's power over the colonies. John Adams, looking back in his old age, remembered:

> It was known that neither King, nor ministry, nor archbishops could appoint bishops in America without an Act of Parliament; and if Parliament could tax us, they could establish the Church of England with its creeds, articles, tests, ceremonies, and tithes, and prohibit all other churches, as conventicles and schism shops.[5]

Adams gives us another reason the colonists did not want bishops. For Parliament to establish Anglican bishops would mean that the religious laws in each of the colonies would be wiped out. Most colonies had, by law, an established church. In some cases it was the Anglican Church, in other cases it was another denomination. If Parliament could establish a bishop for the colonies, it would have gained the power to alter colonial law and faith.

It must also be remembered that a bishop in England had some civil power as well as religious power. For instance, to this present day in England the right to act as a notary public is granted, nominally, by the Archbishop of Canterbury. Were a bishop to be set up by Parliament, his civil powers might be great. Well did the colonists know how Archbishop Laud persecuted the Puritans under King Charles I, and that era was not remote to them.

Even the Anglicans in America were upset; two-thirds of the signers of the Declaration of Independence were members of the Anglican Church. The Anglicans in Virginia had earlier fought for and won the right of their church to choose its own minister and conduct its own affairs, and they knew that, with a bishop, they would lose this power to him. He might even claim authority over all the churches, Anglican and non-Anglican, within his jurisdiction. Behind the face of a bishop lurked the dreaded hand of Parliament.

The British understood the religious issues behind the War for Independence. In fact, the Tories called the Rebels "congregational and presbyterian republicans."[6] Another way in which the British showed their understanding of the religious motives of their enemies was in their treatment of colonial churches. The British troops regularly burned churches, or used their pews for firewood, or stabled their horses in the colonial churches, and did virtually anything to show their contempt. They hated this American Christianity which refused to roll over and play dead at Parliament's command. It would not be too much to say that the war itself was a Puritan/Calvinist revolt. Most of the leaders of the colonies, as well as a majority of the population, were orthodox Christians, mainly of Calvinist leanings.

One point which we must emphasize at the risk of repetition is the conservative nature of the War for Independence. These colonists were not crazed revolutionaries dedicated to burning up and tearing down. This "revolt" was unique for the orderly, legal way the colonists assumed the administration of the government. As George Read, another signer of the Declaration of Independence, pointed out, he was against Parliament but not against the King. Read may have been a Rebel, but there was little of the revolutionary spirit about him in the modern sense of the word. There were some acts of violence against Tories but, on the whole, the reprisals were limited, given the British hostilities against American churches and people.

The Americans were a loyal people, mainly English, primarily interested in being allowed the rights of Englishmen. One surprising fact is that, in the ten years prior to the war, British law books sold heavily in the colonies. This manifested the colonists' concern over doing their business according to law. They had no objections to the law as it was in force in Britain. To this day, in matters upon which no laws have been passed, the principles of English common law are in force in the United States.

We should also note that no one was in favor of total independence until quite late in the conflict. Until May 1776, only two months before the Declaration of Independence was written, the colonists were still hoping that their differences could be sorted out peacefully.

Again, we look at the leaders of the American uprising. These men were not downtrodden, lower-class agitators. The leaders of the war came from the upper class, from among those who already had exercised authority in the colonies. Their status was similar in prominence to modern-day United States senators and governors. These men had little to gain and much to lose by taking their stand. They risked, and in many cases lost, their earthly fortunes in order to stand against the dictatorship of Parliament.

So conservative were the Rebels that two signers of the Declaration of Independence, Richard Henry Lee and Thomas Nelson, Jr., opposed a bill in the Virginia legislature which would have freed the citizens from having to pay back any debts they owed to Englishmen. Although at war with England, Nelson said, "Whatever is voted...I will pay my own debts like an honest man."[7]

In most countries, when a revolt takes place one of the first acts of the new revolutionary government is to dissolve the parliament or legislature of the old administration. In America, far from doing this, the colonial legislatures stayed in power and, as early as 1776, eight colonies had adopted new constitutions in an orderly manner. Practically the only legal change involved renouncing the king and the royal governor appointed by him to substitute for one elected by the people. In fact, it was these very legislatures, along with their representatives in the Continental Congress, which directed the war effort.

Of course, time did not stand still in the rest of the world while the British and Americans fought it out. The period of the War for Independence was also a time of great conflict between Britain and her continental neighbors in Europe. In fact, had it not been for the events in Europe, Britain would most certainly have crushed the colonies without much trouble.

The nation which rescued the colonists was France. Without that nation, America could not have succeeded. As an enemy of Britain, France secretly had been sending aid to the colonies since 1776. In 1778, she came out in the open and declared war on Britain. This was a major blow to the British war effort. One side effect of France's alliance with America was that many Indian tribes were influenced to join in the war on the side of the Americans rather than to support Britain. Washington, reporting to Congress, said:

Being told that France was assisting us, and about to join the war, they seemed highly pleased: and Mr. Kirkland [their missionary] said he was persuaded it would have a considerable effect on the minds of several of the [Indian] nations, and secure to us their neutrality, if not a declaration and commencement of hostilities in our favor....[8]

America could not have won the war without French assistance. While we, as Americans, have a justly high opinion of our country, greatness neither began nor ended with us. If France and England had not been enemies, if France had not been willing to support the Americans, there would have been no United States of America as we know it.

To add to England's difficulties, Spain declared war in 1779, and Holland in 1780. Neither of these nations was allied with the colonies. They were fighting solely for their own interest. Still, it was all a drain on Britain's resources. We see how God made all the events of the era fit together like clockwork to perform His purposes. By allowing a great deal of Western Europe to be at war with Britain at the right time, less attention could be paid to the war in America.

Another interesting aspect of the European situation is that the American War for Independence brought both England and France close to bankruptcy. It was expensive to fight a war on the other side of the Atlantic. In France's case in particular, we can see how one set of events may set off a chain reaction which causes other things to happen. By assisting America in order to attack Britain, France drained itself financially. This economic collapse made possible the terrible French Revolution, which ravaged the French nation. Without meaning to do so, the French monarchy destroyed itself in helping America survive. The United States will always owe the French a debt of gratitude for the sacrifice made at that time, even though made to undermine Britain.

Economically, things were not easy in America during the war, and the fault was not all Britain's. Before the war started the colonies had fallen into the disastrous habit of printing paper money. What had saved the Americans from ruining their own economy was the insistence of the British Crown and Parliament that they print no more. Parliament might not have been acting lawfully in barring the colonies from paper money issues, but the step was beneficial. With the war, however, the colonies reverted to their old practice.

The Continental Congress lacked the power to tax the colonists. How then was it to pay for the war effort? The only course of action was to print paper money and trust that the colonies would back it with hard cash derived from taxing the people. It failed to work. The Continental Congress started by printing $200 million, trusting in the colonies. Instead the colonies, rejoicing in their newfound freedom to do as they pleased, printed another $200 million of their own. As earlier in the century, all this paper money became worthless, and nightmare inflation again stalked the land. One form of welfare the British engaged in was to print counterfeit American money and filter it into the colonies to destroy the value of American money. The British counterfeiting was unnecessary. The Americans were conducting their own economic demolition derby.

As a result, the colonial army was in trouble. What shopkeeper would trade goods for worthless paper money? By all means, they would accept British gold and silver coins. Because the British at this time had sound money, the merchants preferred to deal with the enemy. In response, the colonies enacted legal-tender laws. It required military power to enforce the legal-tender laws, as we can see from General Putnam's order:

> In future, should any of the inhabitants be so lost to public virtue and the welfare of their country, as to presume to refuse the currency of the American states in payment for any commodities they might have for sale, the goods shall be forfeited, and the person or persons so refusing, committed to close confinement.[9]

These legal-tender laws were legal indeed, but not tender!

General Washington complained, "a wagon load of money will scarcely purchase a wagon load of provisions."[10] One officer observed that if he bought a horse it would cost him a twenty-year salary. Inflation thus crippled the war effort. One man wrote that a pint of whiskey cost one hundred dollars, which was also the price of a half bushel of potatoes.[11] In terms of gold, a 1779 dollar was worth five cents in gold. Prices doubled between September 1779 and January 1780, and again between January 1780 and March of the same year. This means that prices rose 300 percent in six months! By May 1780, a dollar's worth of gold cost sixty dollars in paper.[12] Economically, things were becoming steadily worse, even as militarily, thanks to the French, the colonies were close to victory.

The end came at Yorktown, October 19, 1781. Trapped on the peninsula by a combined French and American army, with a French fleet off the coast, Cornwallis did what he had to do—surrender—virtually ending the war.

America was on her own now. Britain, that overbearing parent, was no longer there to stop the Americans from doing foolish things with their money. The land had been ravaged by war and brought low by inflation. Many churches had been destroyed, and the colonies had been a battlefield for some years. More than a few wondered if recovery was possible.

Chapter 5 Notes

1. George F. Scheer and Hugh F. Rankin, *Rebels and Redcoats* (New York: New American Library, originally published 1957), p. 170.
2. Gary North, "The Declaration of Independence as a Conservative Document," *The Journal of Christian Reconstruction*, vol. 3, no. 1 (Vallecit, California: Chalcedon, 1976), p. 102.
3. T. R. Fehrenbach, *Greatness to Spare* (Princeton, New Jersey: D. Van Nostrand, 1968), p. 107.
4. G. B. Warden, *Boston* (Boston: Little, Brown, 1970), p. 174.
5. Bernard Bailyn, ed., *Pamphlets of the American Revolution* (Cambridge: Harvard University Press, 1965), p. 158.
6. Alan Heimert, *Religion and the American Mind* (Cambridge: Harvard University Press, 1966), p. 357.
7. Fehrenbach, *Greatness*, pp. 209–210, 224.
8. Earl Schenck Miers, *Crossroads of Freedom* (New Brunswick, New Jersey: Rutgers University Press, 1971), p. 81.
9. Clarence B. Carson, *The Rebirth of Liberty* (New Rochelle, New York: Arlington House, 1973), p. 141.
10. Ibid., p. 142.
11. Scheer and Rankin, *Rebels and Redcoats*, p. 503.
12. Ibid., p. 145; Miers, *Crossroads*, p. 208.

The Christian Union Established

SIX

The New Spirit of the Nation

In the classic David and Goliath style, the American colonies finally defeated the British Empire. Critics can rightly dwell on the fact that, without the assistance of the French armed forces and the stupidity of the British commanders, the Americans could not have won. All the same, the fact remains that the American high command was intelligent enough to make use of those factors, and determined enough to continue when the cause seemed hopeless. However highly we rate the French help, it must be remembered that France gave aid only when it was convinced of the determination of the colonists, their staying power, and the likelihood of victory with aid. The French decision to help the American colonies was pragmatic and political; France was anti-British but it was also realistic. Aid was given because success was deemed possible and even likely.

Standing on the threshold of its independent future, America was a bit like a child leaving home for the first time. There was self-confidence, joy, and optimism. There was also fear. The former colonies were on their own now. They no longer had the Crown there to overrule them with its veto power. For better or worse, America would now be making its own mistakes, learning by trial and error, and making its own way as an independent nation in the wider world.

The early years were not without their frightening moments. When the French Revolution brought down the monarchy in France, many Americans cheered. They ignored the fact that the overthrown government had given vital assistance to America in her war with Britain.

They mistakenly thought that the French were fighting for the same things in their country that Americans had fought for in their own nation. They were alarmed and disillusioned when France suffered the Reign of Terror, as they saw freedom and the Church as major casualties of that revolution.

For all the fears, real and imagined, of a young nation, America had one advantage: a sense of national consciousness. Fighting against the British, the colonists had drawn closer together. Like adolescents who discover they are no longer children, they realized they were no longer simply English people living in America: they were *Americans*.

The most important influence governing their new identity was their Christian faith. They felt they were God's chosen people. Thomas Barnard, preaching a thanksgiving sermon at the Salem Congregational Church in 1795, put it very clearly. He said that the people of the United States "may...say to each other with cheerful countenances 'We are a people peculiarly favoured of Heaven.' " Referring to the words of Isaiah 5:3, "And now, O inhabitants of Jerusalem and men of Judah, Judge, please, between Me and My vineyard" (NKJV), Barnard declared, "the United States of America are now His vineyard."[1]

The early Americans also had a sense of mission. They believed that God had great plans for using America to bring about the final victory of the kingdom of God on earth, the millennium. Samuel West, preaching at Plymouth in 1777, declared that upon

> establishing our independence, pure religion will revive and flourish among us in a greater degree than ever it has done before: that this Country will become the seat of civil and religious liberty; the place from which Christian Light and knowledge shall be dispersed to the rest of the world; so that our Zion shall become the delight and praise of the whole earth, and foreign nations shall suck of the breasts of her consolations, and be satisfied with the abundant light and knowledge of Gospel truth which they shall derive from her.[2]

In the 1830s Lyman Beecher also set forth this optimistic doctrine.

> It was the opinion of [Jonathan] Edwards, that the millennium would commence in America. When I first encountered this opinion, I thought it chimerical; but all providential developments since, and all the existing signs of the times, lend corroboration to it....There is not a nation upon

earth which, in fifty years, can by all possible reformation place itself in circumstances so favorable as our own for the free, unembarrassed applications of physical effort and pecuniary and moral power to evangelize the world.[3]

One can go further and say, as some scholars have, that without the preaching of the coming millennium by men such as Joseph Bellamy and Samuel Hopkins, there would have been no War for Independence. The Great Awakening preceded that war and provided moral character and faith. The ministers of the colonies held up to the people the prospect that they, as God's chosen people, would win the victory. The British were fully aware of the role the churches played in starting the war—and took revenge accordingly.

After the war, the Christian belief in the millennium was the dynamic power which did much more than give a sense of purpose. It resulted in action. For instance, viewing themselves as God's chosen people, Americans believed it their duty to move westward and settle the frontier lands. They were God's people and the western lands were obviously meant to come under their godly dominion. The great American missionary outreach was another later result. For the present, the rebuilding of burned churches was a real task.

These Americans also wished other nations to join with them. As the original thirteen colonies had banded together in a war for independence, so they desired that like-minded states join with them in a worldwide concern for faith and freedom. Even after America's religious life became less fervent, the idea of America's role, which came to be known as Manifest Destiny, remained, although altered and secularized.

Illinois Congressman John Wentworth, speaking in Congress in 1845, just before Texas was admitted to the Union, expressed his desire this way:

Many of this body would live to hear the sound from the Speaker's chair, "the gentleman from Texas." He wanted them also to hear "the gentleman from Oregon." He would even go further, and have "the gentleman from Nova Scotia, the gentleman from Canada, the gentleman from Cuba, the gentleman from Mexico, aye, even the gentleman from Patagonia [southern Argentina]." He did not believe the God of Heaven, when he crowned the American arms with success [in Revolutionary War], designed that the original States should be the only abode of liberty on earth. On the contrary, he only designed them as the great center from which civilization, religion, and liberty should radiate and radiate until the whole continent shall bask in their blessing.[4]

Make no mistake here. These pre-Civil War Americans were no imperialists. They were not concerned with size but freedom, a federation of free states. These people saw the United States as an alliance of like-minded, freedom-loving states banded together to promote Christianity (at first) and liberty. Note that the Reverend Barnard said "the United States are..." not "the United States is...." He viewed the United States, as did all Americans before 1860, as an alliance of states rather than a nation. Furthermore, these men wanted only like-minded states, freedom-loving Christian states, to join with them. After the Mexican War, that nation had difficulty forming a stable government, and there was talk of joining Mexico to the United States. While America was willing to take Mexico's northern territories, stretching the United States from sea to sea, there was opposition to letting all of Mexico become a part of the United States. One very important reason for this was that the Mexicans were unlike the United States people in culture and in their attitudes toward government and freedom. For a state to be thought worthy to join the United States, it had to have a good character and hold to the same principles. The United States was seen not as a nation but as a principle of freedom in cooperation.

The New Leadership of America

Although America and her leaders remained a religious people with this sense of mission and destiny, ministers of religion were losing their position as the nation's leaders. Up to the end of the War for Independence, ministers provided the leadership necessary for success. Some ministers even suspended their church services and led the men in their congregations off to war. Respected historians such as Alan Heimert, author of *Religion and the American Mind*, and Ernest Lee Tuveson, author of *Redeemer Nation*, believe that preaching was vital to the founding of the nation. The politicians might have shown the practical reasons for war, but the ministers, preaching the inevitable victory of Christ's kingdom, the millennium, supplied the motive and enthusiasm. But with the end of the war, the influence of ministers declined. The churches were often in ruins; some of the clergy were dead, and the reconstruction of church life was slow. The lukewarm churches had been least hurt by the war.

The new leaders of America were the lawyers. This was a profession not much respected in America up to this time. In earlier Puritan New England, it had not been lawful for a man to represent another man in court and be paid for such services. The Puritans were against professional lawyers and very distrustful of them.

This changed with the writing of the United States Constitution. The Constitutional Convention which drew up this document was under the direction of the legal profession. Under the new government, America became a great place to practice law. When Massachusetts met in convention to consider ratification of the Constitution, Nathaniel Barrell was among the speakers who were against approval of the document. One of his objections was that it was too legal and complicated. He said, "...I think a frame of government on which all laws are founded, should be so simple and explicit, that the most illiterate may understand it, whereas this appears to me as obscure and ambiguous, that the most capacious mind cannot fully comprehend it."[5]

To a degree, the problem was that lawyers involved in promoting the Constitution promised too much. Much of what they had said in favor of the proposed government sounded like what ministers say when promoting Christianity. In effect, the lawyers promised heaven in America if only the people would accept their new plan of government. These constitutional evangelists made claims which no man could ever fulfill. As religious men, they doubtless wanted to hasten the promised millennium. As lawyers, they tried to do this through laws and government, a serious error.

Lest one should think these statements rather extreme, consider the words of John Quincy Adams, a former president, on the jubilee of the United States Constitution. He described the American government in these terms:

Fellow citizens, the ark of your covenant is the Declaration of Independence. Your Mount Ebal is the confederacy of separate state sovereignties, and your Mount Gerizim is that Constitution of the United States. In that sense of tremendous and awful solemnity, narrated in the Holy Scriptures, there is not a curse pronounced against the people, upon Mount

Ebal, not a blessing promised them upon Mount Gerizim, which your posterity may not suffer or enjoy, from your and their adherence to, or departure from, the principles of the Declaration of Independence, practically interwoven in the Constitution of the United States.[6]

Adams, let us remember, was a lawyer.

The New Government in America

It would be very unfair and one-sided not to state the good characteristics of the men who wrote our Constitution. The most important detail which must be pointed out is that they were, with one exception, Christians. Nineteen were Episcopalians; eight were Congregationalists; seven were Presbyterians; two were Roman Catholics; two were Quakers; one was a Methodist; one was Dutch Reformed. The one exception was a deist, although a very few others may have had deistic sympathies. Deists believe in a "supreme being" rather than a God with a personality whom man can know through Jesus Christ. Having said that, we see that even the one non-Christian among the framers of the Constitution was not an atheist.[7]

One unusual detail about the Constitution which shows the Christianity of its makers is the total lack of any use of the words *sovereign* or *sovereignty*. In our day, we are always hearing about nations "having sovereignty" over certain pieces of territory, air space, or ocean. The men who wrote the Constitution realized that only God was absolutely sovereign. No government or nation could claim sovereignty or lordship. God is the Sovereign over all the nations, and hence the nations must conduct their affairs according to God's Law. Any nation which does not act according to the Law of God is saying in effect that it is sovereign, it is god. Can a nation stop the wind from blowing or stop the sun in the sky over its "sovereign" territory? These things only the true Sovereign can do, the Lord, whom even the wind and waves obey. To be sovereign means to be able and free to do anything at all. The framers of the Constitution believed that no human government could claim that kind of power.

It is obvious that the men who wrote the Constitution intended the United States to be a Christian union. Christianity was assumed in everything that was undertaken in the founding of our country. The United States was to have no established Church, but it was to be

Christian. The oath of office is a Christian act, taken on a Bible. The British attempt to place bishops over America had led to a hostility toward an established Church. The Christian premises behind all orthodox Christian denominations were taken for granted by the Constitutional Convention.

The Constitution did not specifically declare that the United States was a Christian nation because the authors saw no need for it. It was presupposed. Every nation had its religion and, in the entire history of the world, there had never been a nation without a religion. There had been no such thing as a secular state. It never occurred to the framers of the Constitution that America would be anything but Christian.

The first secular humanistic state in history was France after the revolution. The framers of the Constitution of the United States were horrified by that revolution and its hostility to Christianity. That a Western nation would be so radical as to turn its back on Christianity was seen as frightening.

A major concern of the framers was limited government. The Constitution limits the powers which the federal government has to prevent the United States government from assuming dictatorial powers. This was made especially explicit in the Tenth Amendment, added to the Bill of Rights: "The powers not delegated to the United States by the Constitution, nor prohibited by it to the States, are reserved to the States respectively or to the people." Very quickly, however, some people sought to increase federal power in order to gain certain "good" results. Thus, an element in the population sought the good life through politics rather than evangelism. The goal was reform from the top rather than conversion and change at the bottom. Regeneration was seen as national rather than personal. Unfortunately, part of the motivation behind the desire to give the government more power was religious. Private citizens and societies were active in all kinds of charitable assistance for those less fortunate. Some saw politics as a shorter route to the same goals. Because of the Christian perspective of America, those liberals interested in social-welfare programs had a different motivation than in later socialist countries. Socialists believe that civil government should get involved in social welfare because they view the State as an all-wise and objective agency which should regulate the personal lives of its citizens and provide for them. In America, liberals who started out wanting to do much the same thing did so because they believed such action manifested Christian compassion and love.

One area in which the United States was quickly tempted to expand the government's activity was in financial aid to refugees. Between 1793 and 1794 there was a revolution on the Caribbean island of Santo Domingo. Thousands of indigent refugees came to the United States. A congressional committee recommended that the government give fifteen thousand dollars toward the relief of the refugees. Many members of Congress felt that this was unconstitutional. Ultimately, after debate, the money was voted, given, and spent. This act, done from the highest of motives, created a precedent in the future for the use of federal resources beyond the bounds of the Constitution. During the debate James Madison, who was against giving the money, voiced his fears. He was rightly worried that this act would set a dangerous precedent "which might hereafter be perverted to the countenance of purposes very different from those of charity."[8]

There were similar attempted actions later, not always with congressional approval. In the late 1840s, when the vital potato crops failed in Ireland, causing the widespread "potato famine," massive *private* aid flowed from the United States to the stricken country. Senator John Crittenden introduced a bill in Congress giving five hundred thousand dollars toward the relief effort. His philosophy was simply, "We [the United States government] can do what individual charity cannot do."[9] Private charity, however, had repeatedly proved itself effective in dealing with social need. A lively debate over the constitutionality of government aid raged in Congress. Thomas Barlow put into words the philosophy of those who would govern by emotions, regardless of the law of the land. He declared that, if we could not relieve suffering under the Constitution, "then it was not right to live under such a constitution."[10] Barlow to the contrary, suffering was indeed being relieved "under the constitution," but without involving the federal government.

There were other areas in which well-meaning people felt the government should take a hand. Quite early in the nation's history, inspection of agricultural products was begun. At this time, inspections were mainly carried out by the state governments rather than at the federal level. Products such as tobacco, flour, and meat, especially pork, had to be inspected in some states by government inspectors. The idea that people could govern themselves—or go out of business— faded early.

One rather amusing government project occurred in New Hampshire. Crows were proving to be a real threat to the farmers' crops there. The state decided that the farmers' self-interest was an insufficient motive for local control of crows. New Hampshire introduced a bounty on crows. For each dead crow, one received a sum of money. The problem was that people began to raise crows in order to get a bounty! This was not an isolated example.

There were other like uses of federal power. American farmers objected to foreign exports which could be produced and sold more cheaply than theirs. Congress was asked to increase the tariff on foreign imports. The farmers wanted the government to use the import tax not to gain revenues but to make imports more expensive. Foreign countries imposed like taxes on cheaper American goods, to the detriment of both countries in the exchange.

The worst incident involved guano—bird manure. The guano of birds found on the Chincha and Lobos Islands of Peru was of the highest quality. Peru sold this guano as fertilizer to America and Europe. Some powerful farming interests in America decided it would be much better if *they* controlled the guano trade and reaped the profits instead of Peru. The United States actually tried to claim the Lobos Islands and sent a naval vessel there to "protect" American ships at the islands loading guano. The United States had no right to do this and, happily, withdrew both the claim and the ship. In order to get a lower price for the guano, the government's next step was to place a high tariff on guano, which was sold at prices the United States considered too high. This meant that high-priced guano would not sell in America. Thus, we learned early on that taxation can be used as a form of blackmail.[11]

In every case where the people wished to increase the powers of civil government, the motives were patriotic and high-minded. Who could argue with giving aid to the needy? Who had so little love for their country as to let American farmers lose business to foreign imports? Who could sit still while Peru forced the American farmers to pay high prices for guano? Very few wanted to be unconstitutional or dictatorial. Sadly, well-meaning but misplaced patriotism began to erode the Constitution. Behind this erosion was a growing belief in the power of works of law, of statist righteousness, rather than in the power of Christ in and through His Church and people.

Part of the growing American belief in the power of law rather than in righteousness extended to a belief in the authority of the courts. The federal judiciary was a subject of intense debate during the Constitutional Convention. A number of the delegates, aware of the long history of judicial tyranny in Britain, declared themselves in favor of restricting the powers of the court. But an independent judiciary was also regarded as the protector of the people against the usurpations of possible despots.

Therefore the Constitution mandated lifetime tenure for federal judges, making them free of political tides. Almost from its inception, however, the United States Supreme Court began to expand its authority. It is the final arbiter of all conflicts which it deems to fall within its purview. The creation of the Federal Judiciary was—very definitely—the sleeping lion of the Constitution.

The later importance of the judiciary seems not to have been fully anticipated at the time by the delegates to the Constitutional Convention, for they did not foresee a passive acceptance of judicial usurpation by the American people.

The authority of the Supreme Court to declare an act of Congress void does not come from any expressed provision of the Constitution. It is based upon an assumption of authority that earlier presidents (Jefferson, Jackson, and Lincoln) denied, but that later generations have accepted. The claim of courts to be entitled to settle arguments between king and Parliaments has, of course, a long tradition. But the English Parliament does not allow the courts of England to rule on the constitutionality of its acts, because England has no written constitution, and no act of Parliament can be held to be beyond its authority.

Since the framing of the American Constitution the judiciary—especially the Federal Judiciary—has steadily expanded its power to a degree undreamed in 1787. Through this development, the Supreme Court has become not merely the "guardian" of the Constitution but also the chief "amender" of the Constitution. The decisions of the Supreme Court are now referred to as the "law of the land."

Today, more than ever before, judicial decisions by the highest court break with precedent and tradition and are based upon secular, sociological, and political grounds. An excellent illustration of this is provided in contemporary interpretations of the First Amendment of the Constitution in which the court rules in favor of freedom *from* religion, rather than freedom *for* religion.

New Church Life in America

One area of American life in which government control disappeared entirely after the War for Independence was religion. Up to the time of independence, most colonies had had a tax-supported State church. It was also the church which, at various times in various colonies, the citizens were forced to attend. No other denominations had the same privileges. In the South, the State church was the Anglican Church; in New England, except for Rhode Island, it was the Congregational Church.

Toward the time of independence, rival religious denominations gained some toleration in the colonies. The rival churches had no rights, but gradually they were allowed or permitted to worship separately from the established denomination. In some colonies dissenters were not required to pay religious taxes to support the State church if they could prove that they were genuine followers of another denomination.

Because of the controversy over Parliament's attempt to impose bishops in America, and because of America's distaste for government control in general, State churches went out of style after independence. Massachusetts was the last state to remove official status from its state denomination (Congregationalist) in 1833.

America's churches were now only supported by those who wished to do so. For this reason we call the system of having no State church the "voluntary church system." The churches could now only survive in terms of popular support. Benjamin Franklin thought this "sink or swim" approach a healthy one. He remarked, "When a religion is good, I conceive that it will support itself; and, when it cannot support itself and...[is] obliged to call for the help of the civil power, it is a sign, I apprehend, of its being a bad one."[12] Many thought the churches were doomed without State support, and some predicted that Christianity would disappear in America. The opposite happened. The churches began to prosper. Within not too many years, missionary outreach in rural and urban areas began to increase, and revivals as well. Whereas previously the imposition of religion from the top had been the norm, it now became a matter of growth from the bottom up. From being officially Christian, America began to be personally Christian.

At the same time, Christians began to develop a grass-roots government through thousands of societies. These tithe agencies ministered to the poor and helped the new immigrants to learn English, gain jobs, and more. Almost every conceivable human need was taken care of. When Alexis de Tocqueville spoke of the United States as governed by private associations, he made references, to a great degree, to these many Christian societies. The social financing of the United States was by Christian agencies.

At the same time, the churches were changing. The powers of the congregation had grown dramatically. Even the Episcopal churches now had vestrymen, an American innovation which gave laymen control over their churches. The Baptists, previously a small group, began to grow. Their emphasis on congregational power and the freedom of the local church began to influence all other churches, including the Roman Catholic ones.

Later, under Lincoln, this trend was halted to a degree. To gain control over the border states, Kentucky and Tennessee, Lincoln backed the infamous Gardner Springs Resolution of the Presbyterian Church. This resolution required all Presbyterian pastors in the South to take an oath of allegiance to the federal government or be ousted. (Previously, a local Presbyterian church could control its property and leave the denomination, as could any church of any denomination.) Federal troops were used to remove pastors who refused, on religious or political grounds, to take the oath of allegiance. In later years, with the rise of modernism, this precedent was used by denominations to strip rebellious fundamentalist churches of their properties.

Up to 1860, however, the local church was a powerful force in America. It created a pattern of self-government and local initiative that is today experiencing a major revival. In the United States, the basic unit of civil government has long been the city and the county. In the Church, the local congregation, as the basic unit, provided a training and a standard of grass-roots responsibility and rule which has been basic to the nature of the United States. A scholar of liberal tendencies once referred in a lecture to the Baptist movement in America as the cradle of "millions of troublemakers!" Some Baptist pastors may fervently agree; we can grant that the church is a monarchy, not a democracy, under Christ our King. Given that limitation, the local church is the basic entity in the New Testament and in the United States. The result has been a proliferation of denominations and divisions, but it has also created a rare vitality. The life of faith in the United States depends on the faith of the local church, not denominational hierarchies or interchurch councils. No attempt to assess the vitality of the United States, or its Christian character, can afford to overlook the fact of voluntarism and the local church.

Many scholars are hostile to any notion that America is or was a Christian country. If by that they mean that it was 100 percent Christian in form and substance, the answer is that it never was. However, the fact is that, although the struggle against unbelief has been a constant one with ups and downs and, granted that now and for some time in the past humanism has been in control of our states, schools, and federal government, Christianity is a powerful force which has shaped and is shaping the United States. The United States is a battleground between humanism and Christianity and, while there is no question as to the power and established forces of humanism, even their form assumes semi-Christian guises because of the pressures of grass-roots Christianity. The United States is a Christian country in the sense that our past was strongly ordered by biblical faith, our present feels the growing pressure of Christian standards, and our future under God will be determined by an alert, articulate, and informed Christian people.

Let us return now to the role of Christian agencies. There were so many religious societies and projects that one can cite only a few of the highlights. Many societies concerned themselves with the immigrants. During the early 1800s, thousands of foreigners immigrated to these shores, often without any money or means of support. The churches undertook to help these people and get them settled. It is a little known fact, for instance, that most of the Irish who immigrated to America became Protestants simply because when they landed in America, desperately in need of help, it was the Protestant churches which gave them assistance and companionship. The Presbyterians took the lead in working with the Irish famine immigrants.

Missionary work among slaves was another project carried on by the denominations, done, by the way, with the approval and encouragement of many slaveholders. To quote statistics from one denomination, when the Methodist Episcopal Church divided over the slavery issue in 1844, the plantation slave missions had 18,182 members. The southern branch kept up the work and in 1860, the Negro membership had risen to 207,000![13]

As men began to move west, the Church went with them. Circuit riders, preachers on horseback, would ride from settlement to settlement, cabin to cabin, preaching to the settlers. No pioneer was so isolated that he did not come into contact with a missionary. There was some competition between the denominations, usually good-natured. One observation by a generous Presbyterian minister gives some idea how thorough these preachers on horseback were. He said, "I at length became ambitious to find a family whose cabin had not been entered by a Methodist. In several days I travelled from settlement to settlement on my errand of good, but into every hovel I entered, I learned that the Methodist missionary had been there before me."[14]

These men made up in color what they lacked in theology. Pity the poor tobacco chewer (a judge, as it happened) who was spotted in a meeting by one of the backwoods preachers. "Look at that dirty, nasty, filthy tobacco chewer," he thundered, "sitting on the end of that front seat; see what he has been about. Look at the puddles on the floor, a frog wouldn't get into them; think of the tails of the sisters' dresses being dragged through that muck."[15] Circuit riders were bold men, ready to use both their Bible and their gun as needed!

In the west, churches once again took the lead in education as they had in the east. These dedicated missionaries were determined to bring education to the frontier. Curiously, western Christians did not like an educated ministry. Having a rough spirit of equality, they felt themselves to be just as good as the minister, and they aimed to stay that way. This did not mean, however, an opposition to education. If a man had been educated *before* his call to the ministry, his flock was often rather proud of him. Also, these folk recognized that, in order to get ahead in the world, a good education was a great help. Essentially, they believed in as much education as making a living required, but for frontiersmen a "real minister" was prepared by God, not by a seminary.

A pastor or missionary could be a builder of schools, however, to the delight of his people. For example, western Baptist missionary John M. Peck, in his first three years, founded several churches; he also founded fifty schools and a college between 1817 and 1820.[16] According to one account, 206 permanent colleges were founded between 1830 and 1860. Of these, 179 were started by religious denominations while only 27 were state or semi-state colleges. Even those state-run institutions were almost all headed and staffed by ministers.[17] Sadly, most of the colleges started by the churches are today run by the states.

Foreign missions were not forgotten. In 1849, massive private aid was being sent to Ireland because of the potato famine. Although heavy donations were being made to Ireland, donations to foreign missions were still staggering. The missionary societies of the Methodists, Episcopalians, and Baptists, together with the American Board of Commissioners for Foreign Missions and the American Missionary Association, collectively were giving in that year more than half a million dollars.[18] In those days of hard money, this was a considerable sum.

Did the voluntary church work? Andrew Reed, an English Congregationalist, visited America in 1834, and gave these comparisons. Statistically, Edinburgh had one church for every twenty-three hundred people in the population; in Liverpool, there was one church for every three thousand. But in New York, there was one church for every seventeen hundred people, and in Boston one for every eleven hundred. Looked at another way, 9 percent of Liverpool's population were communicant members of the Church; in Nottingham, 10 percent. He put the percentage of communicants to the population in New York at 13.6 percent and in Cincinnati at 28.5 percent.[19] The English figures cannot compete with the American. On top of that, stricter American membership standards prevailed, and many attended church who were not communicants.

One of the more colorful aspects of western religion was the revival or camp meeting. These meetings were helped by traveling preachers who would set up camp at a central location to which those living for miles around would come. These frontier dwellers did not live very close to one another and had very limited means of communication. This was probably one of the main reasons these meetings drew so many people. It was the big social event in their lives. The people would come and camp out around the tent, where the meetings were held daily. These revivals were real and important, but the educated clergy found them offensive. Without shouting, rolling, barking, and such excesses, the Spirit of God was not at work, according to the evangelists. A simple backwoods people gathered, in part, in a carnival mood, can be ripe for mass hysteria. The dramatic preachers, with a sensational fire-and-brimstone sermon, could hardly fail to get an emotional response. People would fall senseless and act in any number of peculiar ways when under conviction.

On the other hand, some revival meetings were well organized to avoid such hysteria. However, these seem to be more the exception than the rule, or perhaps they were less newsworthy. The west was not the east. It was an untamed place where emotions ran unrestrained.

These camp meetings basically had their origin in the long-running debate between Arminianism and Calvinism. These terms had changed their significance since the Great Awakening. The core issue now was free will. The Calvinists believed you were chosen either to be saved or damned, that is, they affirmed predestination. Arminianism now stressed revivalism and free will. Arminian revivalism now appealed to emotions in order to reach man's will.

It was this form of evangelism, toned down, that was brought to the east by men such as Charles Finney. Many of these evangelists mistook cause for effect. They assumed that if one could reproduce the emotions, one could make God send the revival. Others recognized that the emotions were a side effect, not the essence.

Many ministers barred revivalists from their parishes, holding with some reason that they would make the people less interested in the regular preaching of the Word. One area of New York had so much religious hysteria that it was nicknamed "the burnt-over district." The artificial appeal to emotions led in some areas to very un-Christian results.

One denomination, in colonial days out of step with everyone else, proved to be ahead of its time. The Baptists were totally against State support and State establishment. One of their leaders, protesting the legal obligation to pay a religious tax, objected, saying, why should people pay "to support a ministry we cannot attend, whilst we demean ourselves as faithful subjects."[20] The Baptists stood in favor of the total separation of Church and State. Obviously, during America's colonial period, when the idea of a State church was taken for granted, they were treated as a peculiar sect. It was only after independence, when the idea of a church established by the State was losing favor, that the Baptists really began to flourish.

The Baptists were in tune with the mood of the age during the early years of the republic. They stood for total independence. Not only did the Baptist churches insist upon being independent from the State but they were also independent of each other, although they did meet in loose associations which had no power over the churches. In the dawning age of the voluntary church, the Baptist denomination took the lead. They had long supported the idea of the voluntary church.

If one man could be put forth as representing the beliefs and practices of the Baptists, it would have to be Reverend Isaac Backus of Massachusetts. Backus and his mother left the parish Congregational Church and joined the separate New Light Church. This was in direct violation of the law Connecticut had just passed forbidding anyone to preach in a parish without permission of the parish minister. In 1748, Backus became pastor of the New Light Church in Titicut, Massachusetts. In the same year the parish placed a tax upon its inhabitants for the support of the parish minister. When the tax collector came to visit, Backus refused to pay the tax. While the tax collector was taking Backus to jail, a friend paid the tax for him. In 1752, in Connecticut, Backus's mother and brother were put in prison for refusing to pay their religious tax. These two incidents must have increased Backus's opposition to the State support of the Church.

A few years later, Backus became a convinced Baptist and reorganized his church along Baptist lines. At this time there was much bitterness between the State and the established Congregational Church on one side, and the Baptists on the other. Many Baptists had property taken away from them and were even imprisoned because they refused to pay taxes to support the State church in their parish. Backus joined the grievance committee of the Warren Baptist Association in 1769. This committee was formed to fight what was viewed as religious persecution by the State. Backus now had a platform from which to fight.

How Backus fought for religious freedom and the separation of Church and State is very important for us today. It is now commonly believed that, because Church and State are separate, the Church ought not to get involved in politics. Since the Church and State issue had been fought longest and hardest by the Baptists, their example is important. Did the Baptists get involved in politics or did they remain aloof in order to stay separate from the State?

Put very briefly, the Baptists felt that it was right to fight politically for Christian principles. In fact, Backus felt that the government ought to protect Christian orthodoxy. There was an important difference in his mind between the State favoring one Christian denomination over all the rest and the State defending the general principles of Christianity. He also spoke out on political issues in which he felt Christian teaching was being violated.

In 1773, a religious compromise was in effect in Massachusetts. The Congregational Church would remain the State church to which the religious taxes would go. Members of dissenting sects like the Baptists could, however, receive certificates proving that they were attached to another church and therefore exempt from the tax. Backus and the grievance committee recommended to the churches that they neither give certificates to their members nor pay the tax, the reasons being that the certificate system was not administered fairly, and that it ought to be the right of every citizen not to pay a religious tax. The certificate system simply gave the Baptists exemption from the tax with a certificate, but it did so as a favor, not as a right. To Backus it was an insult to the Church to be dependent on the favors of the government, which could be withdrawn at any time. He obviously felt that there are times when the laws set down by the government should be resisted. Baptists then were certainly more aggressive than Christians today, and more successful in the political sphere.

The next year, 1774, Backus traveled to Philadelphia along with some Quakers in order to meet with the Massachusetts delegation to the Continental Congress for the purpose of asking for religious freedom. The meeting took place at Carpenters' Hall on October 12. The meeting was a stormy one, mainly because the Quakers were forceful and abusive. Because both denominations had come together, the Baptists were tarred with the same brush as the Quakers in the eyes of the congressmen. When Representative Robert Treat Paine returned to Massachusetts, he spread the rumor that the Baptists had tried to sabotage the congress by whipping up the religious issue to cause a controversy.

When the War for Independence broke out, Massachusetts could no longer be governed by its royal charter. Therefore, the colony called a constitutional convention in 1778 to write a state constitution. Backus and his fellow Baptists worked hard to get the convention to remove the Congregational Church as the State church and to give religious freedom to all churches equally. They lost that battle: the church situation was to remain unchanged. The new constitution went next to the towns to be voted on. Once again the Baptists campaigned against its approval and this time won. The constitution was rejected. The next year another constitution was written. Over Baptist protests, the concept of a State church again survived. This time the Baptists were not able to stop the towns from approving the constitution. It would not be until 1833, after Backus was dead, that the separation of Church and State was to be completed in Massachusetts.

Backus was not only interested in the narrow Church and State conflict. During the 1779 convention, which wrote the second state constitution, Noah Alden, a Baptist elder and convention delegate, asked

Backus to draw up a draft bill of rights for the constitution for presentation to the convention. While it was not adopted, Backus's willingness to undertake such a project showed his concern for the political well-being of the state.

Backus was far less afraid to stand up for what was right on all sorts of issues than are most ministers today. We have already discussed the colonial paper-money issues. In 1781, Backus lashed out at the Massachusetts legislature. He said that Massachusetts paper-money issues were worth "but a 75th part of what they were three years and a half ago," and because the colony gave as its reason "that thereby our public debts will be more easily paid! Whereas money was never harder to get."[21]

In 1788, Backus and Samuel Stillman, both Baptist ministers, were elected to the Massachusetts convention called to consider ratification of the United States Constitution. In general, Baptists were opposed to centralized government, just as they were against centralized church government. There were, however, things about the Constitution which Backus liked, for instance, the prospect of the prohibition of any religious test for federal officeholders. In the end, both he and Stillman voted for ratification.

Backus did not understand separation of Church and State to mean that the State should not uphold the Christian religion in general. He was a supporter of laws against blasphemy, profanity, gambling, card-playing, and theatergoing. As to the idea that laws might be passed making attendance at church on Sunday compulsory (providing, one assumes, that no specific church was mentioned), Backus said, "We have no controversy with our rulers about this matter."[22] The Baptist position was separation of *Church* and State, not separation of *Christianity or the Bible* and the State.

One provision in the new constitution of Massachusetts also received praise from Backus. He said, "No man may take a seat in our legislature till he solemnly declares, 'I believe the Christian religion and have a firm persuasion of its truth.' "[23] Here again, we see that Backus approved of the State supporting the Christian faith generally.

So far was he from separating government from Christianity that he sometimes favored giving the government more power than it ought to have. While we realize that this was a mistake on his part, it does show that this doctrinaire Baptist felt Church and State *both* have a duty to uphold the Christian religion generally.

Backus, along with the rest of the New England Baptists, endorsed a petition drawn up by the state Congregational Church in 1790, asking the Congress to establish a bureau to license the publication of all Bibles in the United States in order to prevent the publication of heretical versions.[24] Of course, Backus and the Baptist denomination also went too far when they favored giving the government power to give financial aid to missionaries.[25] In the Baptists, then, we see a well-balanced denomination in tune with the early nineteenth century. This denomination favored the voluntary church when it was unpopular and/or illegal and was ready to take the lead now that the rest of the nation had swung behind its philosophy. On the other hand, just because the State and the organized Church were to be separate did not mean the support of a secular State. Christianity must be maintained, they taught, but without favoring one denomination over another. Christians, but not churches, normally should involve themselves in politics.

The New Social Concern in America

Government, in its simplest and broadest meaning, has always cared for the poor and the unfortunate. Someone has to provide funds for services for social welfare. In the early years of the republic, people governed themselves without interference from the State. The citizens, outside as well as inside the Church, banded together in voluntary self-government to assist the widows and orphans, to relieve the difficulties of immigrants, to provide medical care, and almost every other need that existed. These voluntary societies were usually founded and run by Christians. There was no need for the State to levy heavy taxes for social programs as the people gave generously to the charitable societies.

This system had another advantage; it kept the welfare programs efficient. If those donating to a charitable agency saw that it was inefficient or no longer needed, they would give their money to another society. Under our State-run welfare programs, we are forced to contribute whether we want to or not, despite the bureaucratic and inefficient nature of the welfare system.

The theory behind voluntary charitable associations came from an Edwardian preacher named Samuel Hopkins. According to Hopkins, evil is self-love, and good is loving others. We show that we are truly

Christians by benevolent and charitable works. The greater good of the whole of society, he taught, is more important than the good of any individual. He would ask, "Are you willing to be damned for the glory of God and the greatest good of the whole?"[26] The point of his question was to establish priorities in the mind of the listener.

In the 1800s many segments, first of the Calvinist and then the Arminian churches, began to slide into Unitarianism. The influence of English thinkers, notably John Locke, was important here. Locke held first to a tabula rasa concept—man's mind as a clean slate. Instead of man being a fallen, sinful creature, Locke saw man as neutral in nature. Second, the Bible and its revelation had to meet the test of reason. Third, in his *Paraphrase and Notes on the Epistles of Paul* (1707-1709), Locke held that the simple Gospel had been diluted and corrupted by Paul. Locke prepared the way for the "higher criticism" of the Bible and influenced the men who early led Harvard into heresies and finally Unitarianism. From those early years to 1920, nearly nine thousand American students furthered their education in German universities. Most became American leaders, professors, and pastors of note, and introduced modernism, Hegelian statism, and more into American church and civil life.

At the same time, the earliest phases of the social gospel began with abolitionism and state-enforced temperance movements. Other movements began also, designed to gain desired social and personal changes politically rather than by regeneration and nonstatist action.

During this period other substitutes for the Gospel came along in areas such as women's rights and prison reform. It would be wrong to say that these areas did not need reforming but, as reform fanaticism grew, the remedies demanded grew more and more radical.

One reform movement which did great damage to America was the public-school movement championed by Horace Mann. Originally schools were run privately, either by churches or individuals. Mann declared for State control. As a Unitarian, Mann saw salvation through education, not through Christ. With religious zeal, Mann preached the gospel of public education, concluding with the statement that "it is for our government...to choose." He said:

> If we do not prepare children to become good citizens—if we do not develop their capacities, if we do not enrich their minds with knowledge, imbue their hearts with the love of truth and duty, and a reverence for all

things sacred and holy, then our republic must sweep through another vast cycle of sin and suffering, before the dawn of a better era can arise upon the world. It is for our government, and for that public opinion which, in a republic, governs the government to choose between these alternatives of weal and woe.[27]

Notice the religious language: *truth, duty, reverence, sacred, holy.* Notice his promise of "a better era" with shades of a Christian millennium with Christianity removed. Note his arrogance in stating that if America, still not a major nation in the early nineteenth century, rejects public education, then mankind—not just America, but all mankind—will sink back into sin and suffering.

While Timothy L. Smith, in his book *Revivalism and Social Reform*, plays down the secular nonreligious religion of Horace Mann and public schools, he is forced to admit it in another context. He writes, "Prominent laymen representing several communions had organized the American Sunday School Union in 1830, for the purpose of supplying both rural and urban children with the religious education *forbidden in the public schools*" (emphasis mine).[28] Thus we see that public schools have never been favorable to religion, even 133 years before the Supreme Court banned prayer from them. From its inception, State control of education was an anti-Christian movement. Many school districts made it otherwise, but the intent was clear at the top.

The reform movement which ultimately led to the most tragic end in terms of loss of life was the antislavery movement. Originally, this was a moderate movement made up of people who felt that slavery was morally wrong. Feeling against slavery was as strong, if not stronger, in the South than in the North at first. In 1826, there were 101 antislavery societies in America. Forty-one of them were in North Carolina, 23 in Tennessee, and 6 in Kentucky.[29]

The first antislavery people were quite practical. As much as they hated slavery, they also knew that the problem could not be solved overnight. The net result of sudden abolition would be the creation of a large group of poor, unemployed black people. These reformers favored settling freed slaves back in Africa and/or a peaceful, orderly dismantling of the slavery system at home. H. Richard Niebuhr describes the moderates in these words: "It may be wrong to speak of their movement as antislavery since it was less interested in chastening slaveholders than in freeing slaves and in providing for their education and livelihood."[30]

Not even the sight of a slave auction always provoked the thunder of outraged decency we have come to expect from the stories which have come down to us. John M. Peck, a Baptist missionary, wrote these words in his journal for January 1, 1842:

> January 1, Nashville. Today I attended for a few moments a sale in the market-place. A negro boy was sold who appeared about twelve years old. He stood by the auctioneer on the market-bench with his hat off, crying and sobbing, his countenance a picture of woe. I know not the circumstances; but it was the first human being I ever saw set up for sale, and is certainly not as oppressive, inhuman and depressing as the state of the poorer classes of society in England, Ireland, and many parts of Continental Europe; yet slavery in its best state is a violation of man's nature and of the Christian law of love.[31]

Then came the abolitionists. This group, mainly Unitarian, rose up in righteous wrath against slavery and demanded its immediate abolition. In emotional terms which sent alarm through the South, they spread their gospel of abolition by means of stirring up hatred against southern slaveholders. Interestingly enough, in the South, Unitarians were advising the slave owners to react violently. Ultimately, it was southern Unitarians who persuaded the South to secede from the Union over the protests of the moderates, who were then left with the task of providing leadership for the Confederacy. The Unitarians accepted the philosophy of the European theorist Hegel, who taught that man makes progress only as a result of conflict. It was Hegel's philosophy which was to influence Karl Marx in his theory that violent conflict between the classes was inevitable and desirable. Hence, the abolitionists wanted confrontation, not peaceful solutions, and they worked for conflict.

Moderate people were upset by the abolitionists. Remarks by abolitionist Wendell Phillips in Boston in 1858 give us an idea why abolitionists were disliked. Phillips accused George Washington and Jesus Christ of being traitors to humanity: Washington for giving us the Constitution, and Christ for giving us the New Testament.[32]

Arminian evangelist Charles Finney was originally associated with the abolitionists, but he later broke with them in horror. H. Richard Niebuhr describes Finney's position:

> To him such abolitionists as H. B. Stanton show the spirit and the language of the slave driver and he sees clearly that a moralism which seeks

the kingdom on earth by means other than repentance and faith is driving the church and the world, ecclesiastical and state leaders into "one common infernal squabble that will roll a wave of blood over the land."[34]

How the abolitionists sent money and guns to political terrorists in Kansas to kill proslavery settlers is described in Otto Scott's book *The Secret Six*. Scott gives a blow-by-blow account of the abolitionists' descent into the political murder of innocent people, leading up to the raid on Harper's Ferry by John Brown.[35]

We have room for only one incident that shows the type of men the abolitionists were. On May 26, 1854, in Boston, the Unitarian Reverend Thomas Wentworth Higginson, under the transparent alias of "Higgins," bought a supply of axes before attending an evening meeting at Faneuil Hall to protest the jailing of runaway slave Anthony Burns. The men at the meeting were finally goaded into attacking the jail to release the prisoner. In the unsuccessful riot, one innocent guard was killed.

Well-meaning charity, loosed from Christian principles, ultimately developed into something ugly enough to spark the War Between the States.

At about the same time as that war, every modern state, including Czarist Russia, *peacefully* abolished serfdom or slavery. Some nations had a higher ratio of slaves than the United States. Only America went to war over the issue because the American Hegelians believed a war was necessary. Their demand for confrontation politics still haunts us and is basic to our politics and problems.

Confrontation or conflict politics unites with another faith—the political belief in salvation from the top down by works of law. The voluntary-church movement believes in solutions from the ground up, in salvation by Jesus Christ and His power and Spirit at work in the lives of men. These two powerful forces are at work in the United States. As nowhere else, they stand in contradiction to each other. The confrontation politics of today seek the steady obliteration of Christianity by humanism. The voluntarist movement of Christians seeks the conversion of the humanists, and it seeks to bring all things in America and abroad under the glorious reign of Jesus Christ, who is Lord of lords and King of kings.

1. Ernest Lee Tuveson, *Redeemer Nation* (Chicago: University of Chicago Press, 1968), p. 31.
2. James West Davidson, *The Logic of Millennial Thought* (New Haven: Yale University Press, 1977), p. 250.
3. Conrad Cherry, *God's New Israel* (Englewood Cliffs, New Jersey: Prentice-Hall, 1971), p. 120.
4. Frederick Merk, *Manifest Destiny and Mission in American History* (New York: Alfred A. Knopf, 1963), p. 28.
5. Rebecca Frumer, *American Nationalism* (New York: Capricorn Books, 1970), p. 39.
6. George E. Probst, *The Happy Republic* (New York: Harper, 1962), p. 105.
7. William Warren Sweet, *Religion in the Development of American Culture* (New York: Charles Scribner's Sons, 1952), p. 85.
8. Merle Curti, *American Philanthropy Abroad* (New Brunswick, New Jersey: Rutgers University Press, 1963), p. 10.
9. Ibid., p. 46.
10. Ibid., p. 45.
11. Paul W. Gates, *The Farmer's Age* (New York: Holt, Rinehart, and Winston, 1960), pp. 327–329.
12. Edwin Scott Gaustad, *Religious History of America* (New York: Harper & Row, 1966), p. 120.
13. Sweet, *American Culture*, pp. 270–280.
14. Ibid., p. 117.
15. George Dangerfield, *The Era of Good Feelings* (New York: Harcourt, Brace & World, 1952), p. 114.
16. Henry C. Vedder, *A Short History of the Baptists* (Philadelphia: American Baptist Publication Society, 1907), p. 325.
17. Sweet, *American Culture*, p. 165.
18. Curti, *Philanthropy*, p. 143.
19. Article by Andrew Reed in *The Voluntary Church*, Milton B. Powell, ed. (New York: Macmillan, 1967), p. 103.
20. Gaustad, *Religious History of America*, p. 128.
21. William G. McLoughlin, *New England Dissent, 1630–1833* (Cambridge: Harvard University Press, 1971), vol. 2, p. 777.
22. William G. McLoughlin, ed., *Isaac Backus on Church, State, and Calvinism—Pamphlets 1754–1789* (Cambridge: Belknap Press of Harvard University Press, 1968), pp. 49–50.
23. Ibid., p. 50.
24. Ibid., p. 51.

25. Ibid., p. 51; see also McLoughlin, *New England Dissent*, vol. 1, pp. 272–273.
26. Sweet, *American Culture*, p. 236.
27. Alice Felt Tyler, *Freedom's Ferment* (New York: Harper, 1962), p. 239.
28. Timothy L. Smith, *Revivalism and Social Reform* (New York: Abingdon Press, 1957), p. 40.
29. William Warren Sweet, *Religion on the American Frontier: vol. 2, The Presbyterians* (New York: Harper, 1939), p. 101.
30. H. Richard Niebuhr, *The Kingdom of God in America* (New York/Chicago: Willett, Clark, 1937), p. 121.
31. Gaustad, *Religious History of America*, pp. 189–190.
32. Smith, *Revivalism*, p. 180.
33. Tyler, *Freedom's Ferment*, p. 508.
34. Niebuhr, *Kingdom of God*, p. 158.
35. Otto Scott, *The Secret Six* (New York: Times Books, 1979).
36. Ibid., pp. 9–15.

From Chaos to Centralization

SEVEN

The War Between the States had changed the United States into a different nation from what it had been. Before the war the individual states had governed themselves in most matters. That system was broken forever when the abolitionists successfully involved the federal government in overruling the states on the matter of slavery. The most obvious example of new federal power was the occupation of the South after the war. While President Andrew Johnson wanted to have the southern states readmitted to the Union, with state governments set up as quickly as possible, the powerful radical Republicans had other ideas. The radicals, who had control of Congress, wanted to prolong the agony of the South. Federal troops remained in control of the South, administering the policies dictated by Congress.

It was only to be expected that, having once exercised great power over the states, the federal government would not be averse to making a habit of it. Of course, the power of the central government grew very slowly during the period 1865 to 1914, but this was the period when the foundations were laid for federal power as we know it today. For the first time, congressional committees began to investigate matters such as the living and working conditions of the laboring class. The government began to look at industrial monopolies, called "trusts," and ultimately set about to destroy them. Americans who had lived before 1860 would have had difficulty recognizing the United States as the same nation they had known. Congressional committees began to exercise star-chamber powers.

The War Between the States brought about other changes, too, especially for the South. The southern economy was wrecked. Southern manpower had also been wasted, with large numbers killed or disabled. Due to the depressed condition of their region, young men in the South desiring to get ahead in the world found they had to move out of the region and head west. This was a further blow to the well-being of the South. The South's anguish at losing a generation finds voice in the plea of the editor of a Texas newspaper: "Don't go to California or anywhere else. Stay where you are, or, if you are anxious for a change, make the change *in* Texas, not *out* of it."[1]

The new America was also to rise out of suffering and new situations to present to the world a different face from the one it had before. It was a time of opportunity, of rapid advance. It was a time when the old days were being left behind, for better or for worse, and a new life-style was emerging. It is to this era that we now turn our attention.

Society

The great industrial development in America, to be discussed later, made fortunes for businessmen who had not been prominent before. This new group of upper-class industrialists developed what was then called "high society." In modern terms, perhaps we could call them the "jet set." This society was based on money and family. Family dynasties like the Rockefellers and the Vanderbilts arose, having more money than we can imagine. It is to be noticed, however, that the older families, who had been prominent before the war, in general did not join in with this high-living group. This group, with enough money to do as it pleased, indulged itself in every way possible.

Most of these families built great mansions. For example, by the middle of the 1880s the Vanderbilt clan owned seven mansions on the west side of Fifth Avenue in New York. The cost of these mansions was estimated at $12 million in 1880s money, a time of hard money. This, however, did not exhaust the money for houses that was available to the family. Their estate in Asheville, North Carolina, was almost beyond belief. This palace, called the Biltmore, had forty master bedrooms, a library with 250,000 volumes, and many other huge and luxurious rooms. The estate itself grew to cover 203 square miles.[2] Other families also built huge mansions and estates for themselves.

Parties were royal in scope, but few could match one held by Randolph Guggenheimer for forty guests at the Waldorf Astoria in 1899. The dining room was transformed into a garden, complete with plants, hedges, and songbirds. The floor was covered with green turf. The menu for the evening was, as might be expected, very extravagant. In 1899 dollars the dinner cost ten thousand dollars.[3] Many hostesses prided themselves on being able to serve up to one hundred guests an elaborate dinner on short notice. With upwards to fifty or sixty servants on a country estate, one can understand how this was possible. To many such people, Christianity was at best of minor concern. The mood of the nation at large had lost its seriousness as well. What the people desired now was to enjoy life and to laugh. Frank Munsey, commenting on what would make a successful magazine in the 1890s, said, "I became convinced that both the price and the magazines were wrong for a wide circulation. If a magazine could be published at ten cents and made light, bright, and lively, it might be a different story."[4]

By contrasting the popular literature of the day with what used to be popular, we can get an idea of the mood of the times. In an earlier era, one representative book which was popular was *The Scarlet Letter* by Nathaniel Hawthorne. Hawthorne's novel was, as was its writer, basically Unitarian, but with Puritan morality still surviving as a holdover. Contrast the late nineteenth century's popular novelist Mark Twain. His famous heroes, Tom Sawyer and Huckleberry Finn, were two mischievous, fun-loving boys. This is not meant as a condemnation of Mark Twain. What we learn about the American public by comparing these two authors is, however, that their concerns had changed from high morals to a desire to laugh.

While considering Mark Twain, it is interesting to note that he tried to write a sequel to Tom Sawyer in which the hero goes west. Twain had Tom, a girl friend, and another boy companion join a wagon train. The wagon train needed some adventure, so the author had Indians capture the girl while the men were hunting. At this point, Mark Twain could write no more; there was nothing funny about being a woman captured by Indians and subjected to a degrading and painful death. When Mark Twain came face-to-face with the harsh realities of life, he had to stop. The public wanted humor; Twain discovered that reality in the wild west held very little to laugh about. The public wanted to laugh. Twain's philosophy of humor in fiction was revealed when he observed, "The stories are only alligator pears—one merely eats them for the sake of the salad dressing."[5]

These factors and others show that America was turning from its traditional culture into a society that was frivolous and desired nothing but pleasure.

Changing America and Evangelism

America's public at large had also changed since the War Between the States. Prior to this time, America had had a settled culture based upon a solid British foundation, with Yankee improvements. With the flood of foreign immigrants, American culture was thrown into a state of flux. America was still more literate than Europe, and more intellectually able, but the culture that had characterized the distinctive American way of life was being drastically altered by foreigners moving in, and by changes in Americans themselves.

The numbers in which these immigrants came are truly impressive. Between 1880 and 1910, 18 million foreigners came to the United States.[6] On average, sixteen hundred immigrants arrived in America every day for thirty years. It takes little imagination to understand how such a vast number of people from almost every culture on earth would rapidly change the traditional "American" way of life.

If the immigrants affected America, it is also true that America affected the immigrants. These immigrants were mainly "dirt poor" people, with little or no education, looking for a better way of life. America had no immigration agents who made certain that only the higher-quality immigrant entered the country. America received a huge cross section of the world's poor and unimproved peasants. America was—and is—the world's land of opportunity.

One of the greatest threats to American culture at this time was the loss of Christianity as the basis of national life. These immigrants arrived in America without priests, ministers, or rabbis. They had lost touch, in many cases, with whatever religion they might have had. America was in danger of losing its Christian character.

Fortunately, the Church rose to the challenge. Voluntary agencies worked among the immigrants to help them and to convert them. The aim was to show these people Christianity at work, while at the same time giving them much-needed assistance. While the exact number can never be known, it is certain that large numbers of immigrants were converted and joined the Church, because Christians practiced their faith in very practical ways.

It would not be out of place here to point out that these Christians working among the poor were against government aid. Nathan Irvin Huggins, in his book *Protestants Against Poverty*, summarizes the view of Miss Francis A. Smith, a Christian social worker in Boston in the late 1800s. Huggins writes:

> The people in her district took relief from the [state welfare] Overseers "as a right, and learned to depend upon this aid in youth, middle age, and old age as a legitimate source of income." According to Miss Smith, young people naturally ask, "Why should we join a saving society? The city will provide for us when we are old." Furthermore, public charity was more expensive than private because there was no reform demanded by public agencies. And taxing thrifty people to support the shiftless was neither a good example for young people nor fair to the industrious and virtuous.[7]

These Christians were also careful not to give aid in such a way that family members were relieved of their obligations, as laid down in the Bible, to care for their aged parents. Aid was given to improve them, not sustain them in their present state.

There were also evangelists who held "crusade" or "revival" meetings in cities and towns across the country. Dwight L. Moody was the first of these crusade evangelists, followed by such men as R. A. Torrey, William A. "Billy" Sunday, and J. Wilbur Chapman, men who are still remembered and loved by thousands of fundamentalist Christians today. These men were all as well known by the public at large then as Billy Graham is now, and taking into account the increase in population, their meetings were just as well attended. No current evangelist, however, has yet equaled their influence. Even some of those whose names are no longer well remembered achieved great success in their own time. One example is Sam Jones. Jones traveled around the country from 1881 until his death in 1906, attracting large numbers whenever he preached. His meetings averaged ten thousand people. By contrast, in 1983, the average major-league baseball game had twenty thousand spectators; taking the increase in population into account, Sam Jones had a higher attendance. In one year, twenty thousand people professed to be converted under his ministry. During one crusade in Chicago, eighteen special telegraph lines were set up in the hall to transmit Jones's sermons, to be published in newspapers. As Grover C.

Loud said, "Sam Jones was preaching to an aggregate circulation of two or three million."[8]

There is no doubt that the welfare work done by Christians and the successful crusades of the big-name evangelists kept the urban areas of America Christian. America absorbed huge numbers of those with little or no Christian faith without losing its Christianity. The greatness of that achievement cannot be overstated.

The foreign element was very extensively reached and converted. For example, a large percentage of the population of Sweden migrated to the United States. Although the popular scope of Christianity in Sweden was limited, and the State church poorly attended, in the United States the Swedish people were soon marked by a very intense Christian faith. Many left their Lutheran churches to establish more voluntary churches and to create a "Bible Belt" in the northern Great Plains states. While old-line Americans became lukewarm in their faith, especially in New England, the immigrant churches became the new energy of evangelical faith in many areas. Immigration fed the voluntary church; the immigrants recognized the revolutionary power of this kind of church and were zealous and joyful converts.

Meanwhile, down on the farm...in the west, civilization was shrinking the frontier. However, the wild west was far from conquered. There were still vast stretches of land populated only by the settlers of lonesome homesteads. These settlers were, in the main, ignorant of Christianity, and the work of the traveling ministers accomplished in the far west what had earlier been done in the Midwest before the War Between the States. One minister, having dinner with a pioneer family, bowed his head and said grace before eating. The family was ignorant of God and prayer; the preacher became known as the man who talked to his plate. The west was a mission field, and the lone circuit rider made it God's domain.

Preaching in saloons, crude chapels, and the open air, these preachers brought Christianity to the settlers of the west who were isolated from the rest of the nation, and frequently from each other. These preachers, often uneducated and unrefined, made a poor army for their spiritual war. However, in true David-and-Goliath style, they won. Religion took root in the west; chapels were established, and many settlers were converted. The deep religious faith present in much of the west today is the result of the dedication of the simple preachers a century ago.

Unitarianism

The Unitarian movement as an organized church was in decline during the late nineteenth century. When it was at the height of its power, at the head of the abolition movement, its leaders had had ambitious plans. Unitarianism, which embodied what their leaders felt should be American ideals, was to become the unofficial State church of the United States. The Unitarian Church and its political counterpart, the radical Republicans, would provide the spiritual and political leadership for the nation, or so it was hoped.

These ambitious dreams were not to be. The Unitarians discovered that Americans did not want to give up their old denominational churches to join them. However, infiltration accomplished almost the same goal. Indeed, many members of other denominations soon had more in common with Unitarianism than with their own churches. It was family tradition, the social status of the older denominations, which made the new infidels reluctant to leave their old churches. Although Unitarianism as an organized movement was doomed to be one of the smaller denominations, those in sympathy with it took their beliefs with them into the Christian churches. As a drop of ink in a glass of water, those holding Unitarian principles worked their way into the older denominations, and ultimately, to one degree or another, began to exercise a liberal influence in most churches. Just as true Christianity is meant for the world at large, and not to be restricted to the churches, so Unitarianism began to influence other areas of life. Closet Unitarians began to have an impact on politics, government, and industry. Christian principles were eroded, government control was encouraged, and evangelical Christianity was rejected. All the blame does not rest with the Unitarians. The Christian denominations were also at fault. Christianity had had an easy time of it. It was respectable to be a Christian. Churches became contented; then they became careless.

In earlier years, churches would discipline their members for two types of sins: moral sin and heresy. Those guilty of immorality would be put out of the church until they repented of their sin; then they were received back into the congregation with love and forgiveness. The same was true of heretics, those who believed doctrines that contradicted the teachings of their church. When the Church became lax, all this changed. Members were no longer punished for immorality. In-

113

stead of punishment, followed by forgiveness if the erring member repented, there was nothing but social disgrace. A man could live under a cloud for years, spurned by self-righteous church members. Without discipline and punishment, there can be no forgiveness. Heresy was not punished at all. As the preaching became more comfortable, with subjects such as hell left for the evangelists to dwell on, church members could not identify heresy. The transition from comfortable Christianity to no Christianity at all was a painless one. Those who objected could always join the evangelists.

One major result of all this was the secularization of American life. While revivals touched the man in the street, the men of influence in the nation no longer paid any heed to Christianity or the Church. All the major denominations were also divided by the events of 1860-1864. Only the Episcopal Church voted to reunite.

As an example of the bitterness between Christians north and south, let us examine the Methodists, who split into two churches in 1844. At that time, it took court action before the northern Methodists would surrender all the property belonging to the southern Methodists. After the War Between the States, the northern Methodists again took southern Methodist property, returning it only after an agreement with the southern Methodists in 1876. Bitterness was stronger than love. One Methodist minister from New Hampshire said, "Instead of giving the rebels place and power again, they ought to be taken by the nape of the neck and held over hell till they squalled like cats."[9]

Another reason for the churches' loss of influence was that the nation's press, the only mass medium of that day, had come under the influence of Unitarianism, in fact if not in name. Without sympathetic newspapers and magazines, the influence of the churches had to decline. This is not to say that the newspapers were strongly atheistic or Unitarian. Outwardly they were more conventional than much of the press today and were even religious in a vague sort of way. They still had to appeal to the common man, who was far more religious than his betters.

Charles Darwin

Oliver Wendell Holmes spoke the truth when he said he doubted that "any writer of English except Darwin has done so much to affect our whole way of thinking about the universe."[10] When Darwin published his book *Origin of the Species* just before the War Between the States, he unleashed a false and vicious theory onto the human race, the effects of which were to be far more destructive than the atomic bomb. Darwin and others were quick to reason out the implications of the theory that the human race had evolved from lower orders of animals. First of all, and most obvious, if Darwin were right, the Bible was wrong. Logically, it then followed that if Darwin, using "science," was more trustworthy than Genesis, which had to be accepted by faith, perhaps "science" could disprove other parts of the Bible as well. If "science" could show that something the Bible said was immoral was actually quite good, the Bible must be wrong. Whatever "science" claimed to prove was then more trustworthy than the Bible.

Second, if human beings had evolved from lower orders of animals, why should man have to obey all sorts of moral rules that animals never have to worry about? Why not live like animals and live according to man's "natural" urges?

Also, if Darwin was right about evolution, then everything is still developing. The laws of morals, economics, and religion which were right for our grandparents might not be valid for us. These are but a few of the logical conclusions of Darwinism which he and his followers developed. The consequences for the world have been far-reaching.

Darwinism also fostered racism. It is not commonly known, but his book *Origin of the Species* has a most revealing subtitle which has been suppressed: *The Origin of the Species by Means of Natural Selection, or, The Preservation of Favored Races*. Darwin's book was racist. The title reflects some of the logical conclusions of this book. After all, if nature allowed prehistoric animals who could not adapt to die off and leave room for the strong, adaptable ones (a theory called "survival of the fittest"), then it was logical to accept the conclusion that dark-skinned humans were inferior to the white ones and would either be eliminated or soon die off naturally. No longer were whites and blacks brothers, both descended from Adam. Now the races were considered biologically different and in conflict in the struggle for survival.

It is true that before the evolution theory became well known, some people were considered inferior to others. However, often the "superior" ones would be quite proud of someone "lower" who proved to have the ability to make good in the world. Collis P. Huntingdon, a California railroad tycoon, was very proud and pleased when a Negro porter in his office was able to save and pay for a house out of his small wages. A man willing to work hard and save had Huntingdon's approval.[11] A man could improve himself by hard work. Under Darwin, biology determined whether one was superior or inferior. This view began to replace the older view, which Huntingdon still represented.

Darwinism definitely made the nation less interested in the Negroes; Kenneth M. Stampp, in his book *The Era of Reconstruction*, observed: "The vogue of social Darwinism discouraged governmental intervention in behalf of Negroes as well as other underprivileged groups; it encouraged the belief that a solution to the race problem could only evolve slowly as the Negroes gradually improved themselves."[12] This improvement many held to be genetic, not moral.

There is more. Richard Hofstadter, in his book *Social Darwinism in American Thought*, summarized remarks made to reporters by Herbert Spencer, a prominent evolutionist, on one occasion: "The prospect for the future, however, was encouraging; from 'biological trusts,' he told the reporters, he inferred that the eventual mixture of the allied varieties of the Aryan race forming the population would produce 'a finer type of man than has hitherto existed.' "[13] Senator Albert J. Beveridge of Indiana was moved to express his faith this way: "God has not been preparing the English-speaking and Teutonic people for a thousand years for nothing but vain and idle self-admiration. No! He has made us the master organizers of the world to establish a system where chaos reigns....He has made us adept in government that we may administer government among savages and senile peoples."[14] That part of evolutionary theory which states that the weaker animals die while the stronger survive led to some logical but horrifying conclusions. For instance, Herbert Spencer said society ought not to engage in "the artificial preservation of those least able to take care of themselves."[15]

Charles Darwin himself, in his book *The Descent of Man*, expressed the same thought:

> We civilized men...do our utmost to check the process of elimination; we build asylums for the imbecile, the maimed, and the sick; we institute poorlaws; and our medical men exert their utmost skill to save the life of every one to the last moment. No one who has attended the breeding of domestic animals will doubt that this must be highly injurious to the race of men.[16]

Hofstadter, having quoted this passage of Darwin, continues: "Yet this was not characteristic of Darwin's moral sentiments, for he went on to say that a ruthless policy of elimination would betray 'the noblest part of our nature,' which is itself securely founded in the social instincts."[17] The logical way to reconcile these statements would be to say that Darwin felt it was unhealthy to help the sick and weak, and ignoble to "eliminate" them. The only alternative remaining is that Darwin would have us go away and leave them to die on their own.

Industry

The late nineteenth and early twentieth centuries were exciting times for industry, showing the best and worst sides of America. In terms which a believer in social Darwinism would understand, Victorian American industry showed the inventiveness of primates, the teamwork of bees, and the no-holds-barred conflict of a barnyard cockfight. Industrial production in the North was booming. In 1850, America had produced 631 thousand tons of pig iron; in 1900, America produced 15,400,000 tons.[18] Just between 1860 and 1870 things had changed dramatically. Industrial production doubled in Maine, tripled in Illinois, and increased fourfold in Michigan. Comparing 1860 to 1870, Michigan produced four times as much timber and Ohio four times as much pig iron. There were four times as many rail miles laid and four times as much freight hauled on the Pennsylvania Railroad; three times as many patents were granted.[19]

Modern inventions were being developed everywhere. It is surprising to learn just how long some of our conveniences of the twentieth century have been around. The telegraph was invented in 1849; in 1858 the duplex telegraph was developed, allowing two messages to be transmitted on the same wire at the same time; 1866 saw the first transatlantic cable laid across the floor of the Atlantic Ocean. The typewriter was invented in 1867, railway refrigerator cars in 1875. The list seems never to end. Electric street railways for big cities were developed between 1870 and 1880. The incandescent lamp was invented in 1880.[20] In 1895, Marconi transmitted telegraph signals by radio waves. It was 1900 when the first human voice was transmitted by radio, and on December 17, 1903, Orville Wright took the first airplane ride, lasting twelve seconds.[21] In 1899, a street fair was organized in Emporia, Kansas. An automobile was shipped to the fair by rail from Chicago and proved to be the most popular attraction of the event. It was also the first automobile ever to have crossed the Missouri River.[22]

In contrast to this picture of industrial progress, conditions in the South showed a depressing picture of economic decline. The ravages of the War Between the States and northern policy toward the defeated South had taken their toll. In 1860, Alabama had produced 989,955 bales of cotton, but in 1870 only 492,472. In Mississippi cotton bales dropped in the same period from 1,202,507 to 564,938. Rice growing, once done in South Carolina and Georgia, had ceased. Sugar cane crops in Louisiana grew no more. In Virginia, tobacco growing in 1870 was only one-third of what it had been in 1860. What little manufacturing the agricultural South had done was all destroyed.[23] The stark contrast between the industrial North and the devastated South made it difficult to grasp the fact that both regions were part of the same nation.

The late nineteenth century was also a time when there was a growing conflict between labor and management in industry. There is no question that industrial laborers of this period worked long hours for low pay. Before the War Between the States, Southerners defending slavery had compared the life of a Northern industrial worker unfavorably with that of a Southern slave. Two points, however, may be made in defense of the North's industrial system. First, industrialists in the North varied in their attitudes toward their workers, just as slaveholders in the South showed varying degrees of kindness to their slaves. Blanket condemnations across the board are most unfair. Second, when bad economic times caused massive unemployment among factory workers, the workers learned what hardship really was. There were worse conditions than long hours and low pay.

The late nineteenth century saw the rise of labor unions to defend the workers. One of America's first labor unions was the National Typographical Union, organized in 1850. This was quickly followed by others. The first large national trade federation, representing labor from all walks of life, was the Noble Order of the Knights of Labor, founded in 1869. This was a very interesting organization, and quite different from groups such as the AFL-CIO which we know today. The Knights of Labor was organized as a secret society, along the same pattern as the Masons. Their leader was called the Grand Master. Another interesting fact was that anyone who at some point in his life had worked for wages could become a member. Employers and capitalists, as well as workingmen, could join. Before Darwinism took hold, men considered themselves, to a certain extent at least, brothers. When Darwinism was properly understood, and men saw themselves as just animals fighting one another for survival, the permanent antagonism between labor and management took hold. In time, the idealistic Knights of Labor declined, to be replaced by groups such as the American Federation of Labor, organized in 1886.

Times were hard in the 1890s, deepening the bitterness between employers and workers, between creditors and debtors. In 1890, for instance, almost all midwestern farms were mortgaged to the hilt. The statistics average out to more than one mortgage per family. These family farms were hard hit by the drought of 1887-1897. As if those ten years of devastation were not bad enough, the financial crash of 1893 was the last straw. Many farming families were ruined. This created bitterness in the agricultural Midwest toward the banks and other symbols of the wealthy establishment.

It was during this period that revolutionary movements were sweeping through the world. Karl Marx, building on Darwin's foundation, developed his theory of revolutionary socialism and class conflict. Part of this system, later known as communism, involved the working class of an industrial society overthrowing the ruling class of bosses, putting the means of production and wealth in the hands of the people. This was the sort of talk which had an appeal to the bitter labor unionists. From this point on strikes and disputes turned ugly, with violence breaking out.

One example of this took place in the Haymarket area of Chicago in May 1886. After police broke up an anarchist/Communist meeting, someone planted a powerful bomb, killing seven policemen and injuring seventy more.

This revolutionary movement was not confined to America; it was a worldwide movement. It is interesting to note that, for all the Marxist doctrine of class conflict in an industrial society, it was backward agricultural Russia that first fell to communism in 1917.

Matters in America were not helped by the philosophy of the industrialists. We have Charles Darwin to thank for this. At least two implications of his theory of evolution were to have unhealthy consequences for society. First, if nature meant for strong, superior animals to defeat, dominate, and destroy the weaker, inferior animals, then successful industrialists must be superior in every way to their workers. Furthermore, what nature meant must be good. What philosophy could better cause alienation between labor and management? This philosophy came out in the testimony of industrialist Thomas M. Miller before the Senate Committee on Education and Labor, in its hearings in 1883 on the state of labor and capital. In the following excerpt, Miller is being questioned by the chairman, Senator Henry W. Blair of New Hampshire:

> Senator Blair: As a rule, do you think that the working people devote more time to labor or less time than the employers? A. Less, I think.
>
> Q. On the other hand, I suppose, the working people have less to hope for from the results of their labor? A. That is true, unless they are skilled and ambitious. I find, at least in our city, that nearly all the men who are now capitalists have been workingmen.
>
> Q. How have they come to be capitalists? A. By evolution, development, according to capacity and opportunity.[24]

The logical implication is that those who remain workmen must, by nature, be inferior, not the sort of attitude that leads to good relationships.

Second, evolution teaches that the superior, more able animals are the ones that will survive. Therefore, wealth and power in each generation will go to those who show themselves the most able (or ruthless). This is very destructive to family life. God's plan for man, as outlined in the Bible and practiced for thousands of years, was for one generation in a family to pass their wealth down to the children, and so on down through the generations. The family is the important unit. The implications of Darwinism are that one should have nothing one does not deserve; this destroys the right and duty of parents to pass their wealth on to their children. Second Corinthians 12:14 NKJV says in part, "For the children ought not to lay up for the parents, but the parents for the children." This philosophy comes out, rather subtly, in the testimony of Jay Gould, another industrialist, before the same 1883 hearings held by the Senate Committee on Education and Labor. Gould is being questioned by Senator Blair.

> Q. Of the men who conduct business enterprises and wield the power of capital in this country today, what proportion do you think are what are called "self-made men"? A. I think they are all "self-made men"; I do not say *self*-made exactly, for the country has grown and they have grown up

with it. In this country we have no system of heirlooms or of handing down estates. Every man has to stand here on his own individual merit.[25]

John D. Rockefeller in, of all things, a Sunday-school address, justified vicious business practices designed to put competitors out of business; he found his justification in the theory of evolution. "The growth of a large business is merely a survival of the fittest....The American Beauty Rose can be produced in the splendor and fragrance which bring cheer to its beholder only by sacrificing the early buds which grow up around it. This is not an evil tendency in business. It is merely the working-out of a law of nature and a law of God."[26]

The Reform Movement

If there were those who felt they were biologically superior, there were also the people at the other extreme who sought to impose their version of justice and fair play on others. The reform movement after the War Between the States was a logical extension of the movement in the earlier part of the century. It reached its apex of power in the "reconstruction" of the defeated southern states. Reconstruction in reality was the name of the effort of the radical-Republican-controlled Congress to exact its pound of flesh from the South. The victorious abolitionists were now determined to remake the South in their own image.

The list of abuses is too long to recount here. The highlights include the setting up of a military government over the South until loyal governments composed of Negroes and recently arrived northern "carpetbaggers" could be set up. Although the Republicans had earlier claimed that no state could leave the Union, they now insisted that the southern states were out of it and could only be readmitted on the North's terms. For one thing, before being readmitted, the states had to ratify the Fourteenth Amendment to the Constitution. If only states could ratify amendments, and if the southern region could not become states again until they ratified it, there is a logical contradiction. Reconstruction had more to do with the humiliation of the defeated Confederacy than it did with logic.

One reform the radicals insisted on was that the Negroes be given the right to vote. Former slaves, mostly illiterate, with no education or experience, were in no condition to exercise the right to vote. The possibilities for intimidation and fraud would be infinite. Many northern states refused to allow black suffrage. In fact, only six northern states gave the vote to Negroes; in 1865 alone, Connecticut, Wisconsin, and Minnesota rejected proposals allowing Negroes to vote there.

For many years after the southern region was readmitted as states, the Negroes, aided by northerners who moved south for this purpose, and by local unionists, governed those states. Only gradually were the former Confederates given back their full civil rights. A minority report of the Congressional Committee on Reconstruction stated: "History, till now, gives no account of a conqueror so cruel as to place his vanquished foes under the domination of their former slaves. That was reserved for the radical rulers in this great Republic."[27]

In the end, the radicals lost power in Congress and the white southerners regained control of the southern state governments. Even the great reform magazine, the *Nation*, admitted the mistakes of Reconstruction in a striking passage in an 1890 issue. It read:

> There is a rapidly growing sympathy in the North with Southern perplexity over the Negro problem....Even those who were not shocked by the carpet-bag experiment...are beginning to "view with alarm" the political prospect created by the increase of the Negro population, and by the continued inability of Southern society to absorb or assimilate them in any sense, physical, social, or political....The sudden admission to suffrage of a million of the recently emancipated slaves belonging to the least civilized race in the world...was a great leap in the dark....Who or what is...[the Negro] that we should put the interests of the 55,000,000 whites on this continent in peril for his sake?[28]

Revisionist historians are giving us a much more favorable picture of Reconstruction. They call attention to the good intentions of the leaders of the movement, the new freedom given to the freed slaves, and they rightly call attention to the fact that corrupt politics was not a monopoly of the Reconstruction regimes. Both before and after Reconstruction, southern politics were corrupt and evil. Given the broader view of the southern political scene, reconstruction becomes less evil, and some surprisingly good aspects emerge.

However, the war and Reconstruction left the South economically devastated. Its previously unfavorable position in relation to the North was greatly aggravated.

There was still another problem. Reconstruction represented the triumph of compulsory, top-down, political salvation. It did nothing to further Christian relationships between the races; instead, it led to bitterness, anger, lynchings, repression, peonage, hatred, and more. Both northern reconstructionism and the southern reaction were political and bypassed the Bible as the only sound basis for social and personal reconstruction.

The major reform movement of the late nineteenth century was populism. Populists were in favor of equality for all. They looked at the industrialists with their ideas of superiority and rejected them. They saw the political bosses manipulating public affairs in the cities and were against them. They saw a handful of companies with virtual monopolies over the railways, oil, steel, and other industries and felt it was immoral. They saw banks foreclose on the mortgages of decent farming families in the Midwest and were enraged. Populists were eager to throw down the powerful few from their thrones and establish democracy, with all men equal. It was the populist spirit that promoted the use of primaries by the political parties so that the man on the street rather than a small group of political bosses could choose the candidates for election. It was this same spirit that brought about the constitutional amendment providing for the direct election of senators. Up until then, the state legislatures had appointed senators to Congress. This was an aspect of the beautifully balanced checks and balances of the Constitution; the people would elect the representatives and the state would choose the senators. This way, no brief whim of popular opinion or power play by state officials could control Congress. However, the idea of the legislators huddling together to choose the senators seemed too much like back-room politics by party bosses, to the reformers (and they were often right). But by giving the power to elect the senators, the character of the Senate was changed into a second, smaller House of Representatives. Instead of representing the state and its government, it was subject to public opinion; both houses of Congress were now controlled by the same influence. William Allen White, a populist, was overly optimistic when he said: "Under the primary system any clean, quick-witted man in these states can defeat the corporation senatorial candidate at the primary if the people desire to defeat him."[29] Among other things, White neglected to add that his clean, quick-witted man had better have large amounts of money to spend if he were to win.

As the reader may have noticed, there are points of similarity between our description of Marx's socialism and the populist movement, although they are not identical. Hofstadter described their relationship:

> The characteristic Progressive thinker carried on a tolerant and mutually profitable dialogue with the Socialists of the period, perhaps glancing over his shoulder with some anxiety from time to time, to be sure that Marxian or Fabian ideas were not gaining too much ground in the United States, but chiefly because in this age of broad social speculation he was interested to learn what he could from Social criticism.[30]

To get some idea of where populism was leading its followers, let us look briefly at two books written by a major populist of his day, Charles Ferguson. In 1900, he wrote in *The Religion of Democracy*, "The mission of democracy is to put down the rule of the mob."[31] "A mob is a crowd of people corrupted by unrealizable abstractions."[32] To Ferguson, a mob was a crowd which had a defective set of opinions. And how should a democracy treat those whose opinions are wrong? "Democratic government is the standing together of a multitude of men who could each stand alone. Its business is to balk the mob of the fraudulent gains of a sordid good fellowship and to brace them to moral independence."[33] For Ferguson, democracy did not mean elections. "It is a fond saying that government derives its just powers from the consent of the governed. Just government exists by the force of the self-governing in repression of the unjust. When the governed consent to justice government will have served its time and can pass into the free and unanimous co-operation of the people."[34]

There you have it: Democracy saves us from the mob, and the mob is a crowd whose ideas are impractical or wrong. Democracy means that another group of people whose ideas are "right" sits on the group whose ideas are "wrong" until it evolves into a condition in which they accept the "right" ideas. Then all will agree that we need no government because there will be no one to repress. Ferguson took at least three things for granted in his reasoning. First, he accepted the idea of a group of men who are enlightened enough to determine right from wrong. Second, he believed that this group, because they are right, may use force to impose their ideas on the others. Third, he obviously believed that in the evolutionary ways of things (Darwin again), even those who are wrong will die out or develop to the point where everyone agrees on what is "right."

Ferguson served for a time in the Wilson administration. He saw America try socialist methods. He saw emergency war powers limit the freedom of the citizens for the first time in American history. Then, in 1918, Ferguson wrote a second book called *The Revolution Absolute*. He reacted favorably to the dictatorial wartime powers of Wilson. Ferguson, a champion of "democracy," was excited about the dictatorial power of Wilson. He wrote: "By using his [Wilson's] arbitrary power to crown and accredit the real masters of arts, and to set up new centres of intrinsic power and organized enterprise, it is possible for the President to quadruple the productive ability of the United States, or increase it by some higher multiple."[35] He even advocated government control of the news media. "Under the pressure of war all the nations have learned that the control of credit, commerce and the news-service are legitimate social powers, not hereafter to be given over to the covert administration of a class, under pretense that they are not social powers; yet needing a socialization that is not arbitrary but in harmony with the intrinsic laws that condition the productive process."[36] Ferguson, we should not forget, began as a minister; he ended an advocate of salvation by State power, not by Jesus Christ.

This period, 1865 to 1914, was a contradiction. There were great advances in industry, triumphs of the Christian faith, and the downfall of abolitionists and radical Republicans. Americans had less interference from government than they do today. The standard of living was higher than in Europe; witness the millions of immigrants. It was also a world without the fears we have today. Men had no Soviet bloc to fear, and no atomic weapons. The nation was in no danger of being taken over by a foreign power. Fear for the people of this era was whether or not the bank would foreclose on their mortgages.

It was also the era of Charles Darwin and Karl Marx; it was the time of "reformers" who had no idea of the Pandora's box they were opening. All these things, however, were still in their infancy.

Meanwhile, however, a new force was beginning to grow across the United States. The major denominations had compromised with Darwinism; there were movements into the social gospel, and a statist, coercive, top-down salvation by politics. Prominent pastors and scholars came together to publicize a series of essays called *The Fundamentals*. As a consequence, the fundamentalist movement was born. Many churches separated from main-line denominations to form independent churches. The fundamentalist movement has often been criticized, and it is easy to do so. The fundamentalists' zeal sometimes led them to be too quarrelsome; they sometimes separated from one another, and from the world around them. Some became anti-intellectual, and others divisive. However, when all is said and done, some remarkable facts emerge. It was the fundamentalists who showed missionary zeal at home and abroad; it was their churches which led Christ's flock and grew. Fundamentalists began to command an increasing number of Americans so that, by the 1970s, well over 50 million adult Americans identified themselves as born-again Christians.

And this was not all! Fundamentalism revived what had been flagging in American church life, grass-roots faith and action, voluntarism on a grand scale. This led to Bible schools, colleges, new missionary agencies, and more. After World War II, it led to the Christian-school movement, homes for the aged, homes for delinquents, in addition to other effects. Voluntarism was on the march again, to create a Christian America. This time, however, it was increasingly in conflict with humanistic churches and with humanistic statism.

A country is Christian where the Lord's people are successfully at work capturing and reshaping persons, homes, schools, churches, and civil agencies for Jesus Christ. It is a country in the process of being shaped by the Word of God. No such place exists in perfection this side of heaven, nor will it, but Christians have a duty to claim all things for Christ and to bring men and nations under His saving power. This effort and process is a major force in the United States. The voluntary church is developing and is coming into its own. Its future is as bright as the promises of God!

1. Merton Coulter, *A History of the South, Vol. 8, The South During Reconstruction 1865–1877* (Louisiana State University Press and The Littlefield Fund for Southern History of the University of Texas, 1947), p. 187.
2. Frederick Lewis Allen, *The Big Change* (New York: Harper & Brothers, 1952), pp. 28–30.
3. Ibid., pp. 37–39.
4. Lazer Ziff, *The American 1890s* (New York: Viking Press, 1966), p. 121.
5. Ibid., p. 67.
6. Samuel Eliot Morison and Henry Steele Commager, *The Growth of the American Republic* (New York: Oxford University Press, revised edition, 1960), vol. 2, p. 151.
7. Nathan Irvin Huggins, *Protestants Against Poverty* (Westport, Connecticut: Greenwood, 1971), p. 67.
8. Grover C. Loud, *Evangelized America* (New York: Lincoln Mac Veagh–The Dial Press, 1928), pp. 259–260.
9. Coulter, *History of the South*, p. 332.
10. Richard Hofstadter, *Social Darwinism in American Thought* (Boston: The Beacon Press, revised edition, 1955), p. 32.
11. Oscar Lewis, *The Big Four* (New York: Alfred A. Knopf, 1938), p. 214.
12. Kenneth M. Stampp, *The Era of Reconstruction* (New York: Vintage Books, 1965), p. 20.
13. Hofstadter, *Social Darwinism*, p. 48.
14. Stampp, *Reconstruction*, pp. 20–21.
15. Hofstadter, *Social Darwinism*, p. 44.
16. Ibid., p. 91.
17. Ibid., p. 91.
18. John A. Garraty, ed., *Labor and Capital in the Gilded Age* (Boston: Little, Brown, 1968), p. vii.
19. Morison and Commager, *American Republic*, pp. 10–11.
20. Ibid., pp. 127–129.
21. Allen, *Big Change*, pp. 118–119.
22. Ibid., p. 7.
23. Morison and Commager, *American Republic*, p. 14.
24. Garraty, *Labor and Capital*, pp. 51–52.
25. Ibid., p. 48.
26. Hofstadter, *Social Darwinism*, p. 45.
27. Coulter, *History of the South*, p. 146.
28. Stampp, *Reconstruction*, pp. 17–18.

29. Richard Hofstadter, *The Age of Reform* (New York: Alfred A. Knopf, 1955), p. 256.
30. Ibid., p. 238.
31. Charles Ferguson, *The Religion of Democracy* (New York: Funk & Wagnalls, 1900), p. 85.
32. Ibid., p. 86.
33. Ibid., p. 103.
34. Ibid., p. 103.
35. Charles Ferguson, *The Revolution Absolute* (New York: Dodd, Mead, 1918), pp. 116–117.
36. Ibid., p. 216.
37. Hofstadter, *Age of Reform*, p. 260.

EIGHT

America Before World War I

America before World War I was a very different place from what it is today. Outwardly America has changed as automobiles, airplanes, and televisions have been invented and become commonplace. The greatest change, however, involved America's soul; it was not a change for the better. America had started its life as a freedom-loving confederation of states. Then the cancer set in. At first, the rot was very small and progressed slowly, but gradually it grew more quickly.

Up until the War Between the States, the hand of the federal government was felt only lightly upon the states, and not at all upon the individual citizen. Indeed, most citizens went about their lives hardly aware of either state or federal government, except at election times. Enterprise was free. A man could set out to make his fortune by investing his capital and labor in whatever he chose; the restrictions were few and dealt mainly with enforcing moral standards.

As we have seen, this almost ideal state of affairs was ruined by idealistic reformers and headstrong ministers insisting on having their own brand of morality enforced immediately by the government, at the point of a bayonet if necessary. The War Between the States resulted from pressures brought to bear upon the federal government to intervene in the southern states on the slavery question; Washington was unable to withstand these pressures, and we went to war. Instead of seeking a peaceful elimination of slavery, an aggressive method was used.

Freedom-loving Americans, north and south, mourned the loss of freedom that resulted from the war. The United States government, once set upon the road to great power, would not turn back. The government began to try its hand at intervening in and issuing regulations for commerce, business, and other areas of the nation's life. To those reared in the pure air of prewar freedom, the bell was tolling for America, the death knell of freedom in the United States.

Still, America was relatively free, certainly by today's standards. As Carl Schurtz wrote, "Here in America you can see how slightly a people needs to be governed. In fact the thing that is not named in Europe without a shudder, anarchy, exists here in full bloom."[1] What had happened after the War Between the States was that government and power had been centralized in Washington. This was bad enough in and of itself, but nothing compared with the onslaught of statism which was to follow.

It is a curious fact of history that America and Europe seem destined to learn bad habits from each other. We see this in a rather curious spin-off of American centralization. At the time of the War Between the States, Germany was a loose confederation of kingdoms and principalities. It was America's example of centralization of power that provided the Germans with the inspiration to unite into one centralized state. Without realizing it the Americans, by creating a strong central government, not only influenced their own development but altered the history of the world in ways they could not have imagined. The Germans also learned total war from the American example, 1860–1864.

Europe and America Part Company

America's political heritage began to develop separately from Europe's from the moment the United States gained independence. One way this difference can be illustrated is by comparing the European revolutions of the late eighteenth and early nineteenth centuries with the American Revolution.

Historians who insist on using words only according to their precise definitions do not approve of calling our War for Independence the "American Revolution." A revolution, they argue, is when the old order is overthrown and a new order is set up. In the case of America, the old order consisted of the American colonies being governed by their own legislatures, with the king of England as their head of state. The new order which was nearly imposed on the colonies was one in which England's Parliament would be able to act as a legislature for the colonies and pass laws and raise taxes. This change was attempted by Parliament with the full support of King George III's ministers. This, in effect, was an attempted revolution, a new order forced in and the old order forced out. What the Americans did was, at first, to fight for the old order. When their head of state supported Parliament, the colonists took that to mean that he abdicated as their ruler under the old order. From that point on, they fought for the old order still, with the exception that the colonists would have to make other provisions regarding a head of state. Sticklers for accuracy prefer to call this war the "Conservative Counterrevolution": *conservative*, in that the colonists were defending the status quo: *counterrevolution*, in that they were countering the revolutionary new order which king and Parliament were forcing upon them. As a result, we have consistently referred to the war as America's War for Independence.

Europe's revolutions were quite different. They were revolutions in the true sense. However, while America's war kept the new nation going in the direction of freedom and limited government, Europe's revolutionaries took the continent in an entirely different direction.

The size and scope of the French Revolution gives us a good case in point. The French Revolution was started by high-minded reformers against the alleged corruption of the monarchy. However high-sounding the idealistic founders of this movement were, the results were horrifying.

The philosophy which laid the foundation for the horror that was revolutionary France was summed up well by Robespierre when he said, "The People are the Law."[2] This idea contradicts the Christian teaching that God, as Creator, is the One who dictates right and wrong and, therefore, the principles of law by which men are to govern themselves. When an all-wise, all-powerful God lays down the principles of law, peace and prosperity are the result; when the State, claiming to represent the people, undertakes to formulate its own morality, ethics, and law, the result is confusion, distress, and disaster for all.

Many of the measures taken by the revolutionists in charge of France in that era are familiar to us today. The State, trying to act as the god of the French nation, instituted, among other things, an income tax and universal compulsory education for the children, funded by the State.

The French State decreed that life throughout the "republic" must be uniform. Otto Scott describes this attempt to play God:

> France was a crazy-quilt of towns, villages, former principalities and antique kingdoms, cities, and duchies. The Assembly swept all these, with their connotations of the past, away, and placed a mathematical grid, as exact as so many squares on a tiled floor, atop the nation. When it finished it had created eighty-three Departments, 4,770 Cantons, and 41,007 Municipalities. Each had an internal administrative structure exactly the same as its neighbor. In true scientific fashion, names that stretched back to the times of the Romans were eliminated; each department, canton, and municipality was to be known by its number. Plans were already underway to erase the individual cultures, dialects, and customs of these areas; differences would no longer be tolerated.[3]

Not surprisingly, many freedom-loving Americans recoiled from France in abhorrence. At first they had cheered the French Revolution, considering the French struggle to be the European counterpart of the American War for Independence. However, as they saw, with growing dismay, the French State abolishing the Church (becoming, as we have said, the first truly secular State), managing the lives of the French people in a way no mortal man has a right to, and killing great numbers of people to maintain this divine order, the reaction became hostile.

Europeanization of America

America was not to be spared from the new trends in Europe. When these movements arrived in America they wore the same disguise as in Europe, the disguise of reform. In the late nineteenth century, it is true that political machines and big business had engaged in corruption. There were cases in which poor workers were exploited and business competition stifled. The Progressives pointed with repugnance to these abuses; the reformers ultimately were able to so shock the American people that they were prepared to give the government great power to fight the forces of corruption.

One early example of reform as a means of establishing statist power involved a speech by the famous Progessive Theodore Roosevelt. Speaking in Columbus, Ohio, in 1912, Roosevelt gave his three-point plan for destroying "the corrupt political machine" in Washington.

First of all, he favored the initiative: the right of the people to produce their own laws. Second, he favored the holding of national referendums: the right of the people to force the government to accept popular measures. Third, he favored giving the people the right to recall government officials, the ability to remove unpopular leaders. Roosevelt's speech alarmed Senator Henry Cabot Lodge. For the people to be able to bypass the Congress and make their own laws was dangerous, he held, declaring, "The decline of the law-making body resulted ultimately in the rise of the executive...the plebiscite itself was the favorite tool of dictators, be he Caesar or Louis Napoleon."⁴ Both failed to see that neither Congress nor the people have the remedy for sin, and political corruption is simply a form of sin. The search for political answers to moral problems began to aggravate the problems. President Woodrow Wilson was a dedicated political reformer, given to top-down remedies. It was this New Jersey college professor who played the pivotal role in turning America from a nation that was still relatively free into a land of governmental interventionism.

Because Wilson was so significant a figure, it is necessary to understand his character. His faith in his own righteousness and goodness knew no bounds. Other Progressives might ridicule their conservative opponents, but Wilson looked upon them as morally inferior to himself. He doubted that a truly good man could oppose him. In a Christlike pose, he in effect commanded Satan, as represented by his enemies, to get behind him.

If Wilson could lay claim to the virtue, however misdirected, of righteousness, the same could not be said of humility. Wilson was a very class-conscious man: doubtless, this was related to his profound admiration for Britain and all things British. The invention of the automobile and its growing popularity among all classes of Americans upset him. Up to then, it was only the rich upper class who could easily travel long distances; now everyone could. For Wilson, the working classes ought not to travel; they ought to remain at home and work as befitted their station in life.

Wilson was also a very proud man. During the last months of his presidency, while he was an invalid in the White House, the Senate hotly debated whether America should join the League of Nations; this was something Wilson passionately favored. This proposal failed, mainly due to Wilson's unwillingness to compromise. As Otto Scott describes it, "...he refused to accept minor changes in the League of

Nations agreement, and forbade his supporters in Congress to vote for them when the issue was joined. In the end, he chose to scuttle, rather than alter by a single sentence, an agreement he insisted would insure universal peace."[5] If Wilson could not be the peacemaker and redeem the world for mankind in exactly the way he saw fit, then he was ready to see it perish.

One other area of Wilson's personality has to be explored, one which influenced his actions as president in a profound way. Woodrow Wilson had a deep love and admiration for Great Britain. He took his holidays there, drank deeply at the fountain of British culture, and sought to imitate that nation as his ideal. In general terms, there is nothing wrong with that: America contains many thousands of Anglophiles. With Wilson, the difficulty was that it influenced the way he acted as president.

One relatively minor manifestation of his love for Britain was that he desired to imitate, as much as he could, the British prime minister. To further this fantasy, the president established the tradition of appearing to speak before the sessions of Congress. No president since the time of Jefferson had done this. However, since the prime minister was a member of the House of Commons and dictated his government's policy from the floor of the House, so would he. Every president from his day to ours has followed the tradition of appearing before Congress.

More serious, however, was that Wilson's admiration for the United Kingdom caused America to violate its neutrality during World War I and ultimately became deeply involved. At the outbreak of the war in 1914, the people of the United States were anxious not to be drawn into the European conflict. To this end, America declared itself neutral and noncombatant. In fact, in 1916, Wilson fought and won a hard battle for reelection on the slogan, "He kept us out of war."

Wilson made certain that the way America acted as a neutral was more favorable to Great Britain than to Germany. In point of fact, Wilson violated America's neutrality to the point of covertly sending arms to Britain.

The most tragic example of this, because it involved the deaths of hundreds of civilians, was the sinking of the *Lusitania* on May 7, 1915. The *Lusitania* was a British ocean liner which had sailed from New York to England with over eighteen hundred people aboard. According to international law, unarmed merchant vessels are not to be fired upon. Therefore, in the minds of the passengers on board, they were

134

safe. Unfortunately for those on board, things were not what they seemed. In the first place, on the orders of Winston Churchill, First Lord of the Admiralty, the *Lusitania* had indeed been armed and thus lost its legal immunity. English historian and journalist Colin Simpson writes:

...on March 16, 1914, a proud Mr. Churchill could announce to the House of Commons that "some forty British merchant ships had been defensively armed." The term "defensively" as applied to all the Cunarders must be construed as "politician's license," since each vessel could mount a heavier broadside than the Bacchante or E class cruisers then charged with the defense of the Channel.[6]

In the second place, and more to the point, there is circumstantial evidence that the *Lusitania* had been loaded with munitions intended for Great Britain. This, too, would have caused the *Lusitania* to have lost its legal immunity from attack. the most damning piece of evidence is that after the explosion of the German torpedo, there was immediately a second explosion, noted by those on board the *Lusitania* and also those on board the U-boat which fired the fatal torpedo. Simpson, commenting on the second explosion, says:

Whatever the cause of the second explosion, it was not the boilers and it occurred farther forward, was larger than the first, and did far more damage. Nor was it a second or third torpedo. Expert opinion—physical examination and Schwieger's log and torpedo inventory—confirm that. It is probable that the still-sealed records of Captains Hall and Gaunt at the Admiralty provide the only definite clue to its cause. The Admiralty's consistent and adamant refusal—even though by the thirty-year rule these records could be officially disclosed—tends to confirm that the second explosion was caused by a contraband and explosive cargo which was forbidden by American law and which in any event should never have been placed on a passenger liner. The result of Schwieger's torpedo was the flooding of the starboard coal bunkers and a 15 degree list. The result of the second explosion was the sinking of the *Lusitania*.[7]

Anthony C. Sutton, another British writer, says that, in the light of the evidence, the blame ought not to be placed upon the captain of the *Lusitania* as the official inquiry did. He states, "The blame is more fairly to be attributed to President Wilson, 'Colonel' House [Wilson's close adviser], J. P. Morgan [American manufacturer], and Winston

Churchill; this conspiratorial elite should have been brought to trial for willful negligence, if not treason."[8] It would be no mistake to call President Wilson's admiration for England a fatal fascination; over one hundred American citizens died, as well as hundreds of others, because Wilson wanted to support England by fair means or foul.

Wilson confused his own opinions with Christianity—in the sense that he believed himself ordained to change the world—his own way. He called upon Christianity when it might be to his advantage to do so. For instance, he quoted Scripture to back up his program of military preparedness; he cited Ezekiel 33:6: "But if the watchman sees the sword coming and does not blow the trumpet, and the people are not warned, and the sword comes and takes any person from among them, he is taken away in his iniquity; but his blood will I require at the watchman's hand" (NKJV).

With the entry of the United States into World War I, America caught up with Europe in its abuse of individual freedom. In Western Europe it is not surprising that in times of war, the nations will set up emergency wartime governments which curtail certain liberties. Indeed, British historian Paul Johnson goes so far as to say, "Wartime Russia in the last years of the czars was in some ways more liberal than Britain and France under wartime regulations."[9]

Up until this point, America, in times of war, with the exception of Lincoln's years, had never had a repressive government. Wilson, with his European ideas, changed all that. As an example, there is the Sedition Act of 1918. According to Paul Johnson, this act "punished expressions of opinion which, irrespective of their likely consequences, were 'disloyal, profane, scurrilous or abusive' of the American form of Government, flag or uniform; and under it Americans were persecuted for criticizing the Red Cross, the YMCA and even the budget."[10]

One of the persons convicted under this act was socialist leader Eugene Debs. Debs was convicted of treason for giving an antiwar speech before a convention of socialists in Canton, Ohio. Most of the speech repeated standard socialists views on the evils of capitalism and the economic causes of the war. Debs did not speak exclusively to potential draftees, nor did he explicitly urge violation of the draft laws. Yet the Supreme Court ruled that (in the words of Oliver Wendell Holmes) " 'if a part of the manifest intent of the more general utterance was to encourage those present to obstruct the recruiting service...the immunity of the general theme may not be enough to protect the speech." Debs was packed off to the federal penitentiary in Atlanta, a martyred hero of the opponents of war, who helped give him nearly 1 million votes for president in the election of 1920, even while he languished in his cell." (Wilson refused to release Debs during the 1920 campaign: it remained for newly elected conservative Republican Warren G. Harding to pardon Debs—on his own initiative.)[11]

Dr. David M. Kennedy, an authority on the Wilsonian administration, said of President Wilson:

A friend of free speech in theory, he was in fact a foe....He persistently ignored pleas to speak against attacks on German-Americans. He personally approved the high-handed scheme to raid IWW's halls in September 1917, breaking the back of the nation's largest industrial union by mass trials and imprisonment of its leadership....He chafed at the imperfections of the Espionage Act before the amendments of May, 1918, lamenting that the Act did not strictly permit prosecuting opponents of the conscription law "unless they stand in the way of the administration of it by any overt acts or improper influences." On one occasion he told his cabinet that a man who had been overheard wishing for Secretary of War Newton D. Baker's premature demise "ought to be punished if seditious and otherwise be brought here by the Attorney General and given the 33rd degree [beaten] and then the story of his comment given to the public so he would be forever damned by the people.[12]

In this heady atmosphere of power, Colonel House thought nothing of advising a limitation on the freedom of speech regarding Russia after the Bolshevik Revolution. Antony Sutton describes this incident: "As early as November 28, 1917, Colonel House cabled President Woodrow Wilson from Paris that it was 'exceedingly important' that U. S. newspaper comments advocating that 'Russia should be treated as an enemy' be 'suppressed.'"[13]

Voices, alas, too few, were raised against the repressive measures of the Wilson administration. On July 23, 1920, Walter Lippmann, in a letter to his wartime boss, Secretary of War Newton Baker, wrote:

...it is forever incredible that an administration announcing the most spacious ideals in our history should have done more to endanger fundamental American liberties than any group of men for a hundred years....They have instituted a reign of terror in which honest thought is impossible, in which moderation is discountenanced and in which panic supplants reason.[14]

H. L. Mencken, writing in the Baltimore *Evening Sun* in 1920, accused Wilson's Justice Department of maintaining

> a system of espionage altogether without precedent in American history, and not often matched in the history of Russia, Austria and Italy. It has, as a matter of daily routine, hounded men and women in cynical violation of their constitutional rights, invaded the sanctuary of domicile, manufactured evidence against the innocent, flooded the land with agents and provacateurs, raised neighbor against neighbor, filled the public press with inflammatory lies and fostered all the worst poltrooneries of sneaking and malicious wretches.[15]

No, Lippmann and Mencken were not conservatives, and yes, they were writing about America.

Wilson also flouted the Constitution by sending conscripted troops outside the country for the first time in the nation's history. This is clearly unconstitutional. Article One, Section Eight of the Constitution reads in part: "The Congress shall have power...to provide for calling forth the militia to execute the laws of the Union, suppress insurrections and repel invasions."[16] At the time the Constitution was written, the word *militia* referred to a conscripted army. The passage dealing with the militia which we have quoted gives us the three functions which conscripted troops may be called upon to perform. Conscripts may be used to supplement the law-enforcement agencies in enforcing federal law. They may also be used to put down a revolt against the government, and to fight off an attempted invasion of United States territory by foreign powers. None of these three functions here listed authorizes the government to send *conscripted* troops overseas or outside the territory of the United States. This prohibition was respected by the United States government up until World War I; Wilson changed all that.

Commenting on the implementation of the 1917 Selective Service Act, Samuel Eliot Morison and Henry Steele Commager write:

> Congressional leaders, recalling the New York draft riots of 1863, prophesied that conscription would be attended by "rioting all over the United States," and that "we will never get a conscript on the firing line in France," but all these predictions proved mistaken. When the registration offices closed at sundown of 5 June, 9,586,508 men had registered and nowhere had there been the slightest disorder or opposition."[17]

The chilling lesson that Wilson learned from this experience was that Americans are slow to recognize and fight a threat to their constitutional rights and liberties.

Other Wilson measures were received either with indifference or enthusiasm. The people cheered when the Sixteenth Amendment to the Constitution was ratified, authorizing the government to levy an income tax. The people were delighted that the tax burden was shifted, as they were told, from the poor to the rich. They did not realize that they were seeing a socialistic redistribution of the nation's wealth. By forcing the wealthy to pay a greater percentage of their earnings in taxes than the poorer taxpayers, the government was confiscating the property of the rich in favor of the poor just as surely as Lenin was to do it in the Soviet Union. Being successful and prosperous did not become a crime as such, but the government in effect imposed a heavy fine as a penalty for being well off. Like all socialist reforms, the income tax did not long relieve the tax burden of the poor. The very class that cheered the income tax now suffers under it the same as the wealthy.

Less understood by the people but just as deadly was the Federal Reserve Board which Wilson set up. This board, along with its member banks, formed a dictatorship over the American banking system. This elite committee was given the power to regulate America's money supply and lay down the rules which the banks were now forced to obey, all this to be done by an unelected board independent of any control. This happened without a shot being fired.

One man, William Jennings Bryan, a Progressive Democrat and Wilson's secretary of state, forcefully opposed Wilson's devious actions, especially in the field of foreign relations. Bryan was a devout Christian and three-time Democratic candidate for president. While he was by no means a fiscal conservative, he had a keen moral awareness of right and wrong. Shortly before his death in 1925 he was to be the main prosecution witness in the celebrated Scopes Monkey Trial, in which he championed the cause of the creationists who believed the Bible's account of the Creation as opposed to Darwin's theory of evolution.

Bryan felt he had to take a stand against the president over America's reaction to the *Lusitania* incident. Wilson was determined to send a harsh note of protest to the German government about their attack on an "unarmed" merchant ship contrary to the rules of international law. Bryan pointed out that Wilson should also send a protest note to

139

Great Britain over their arming of merchant ships, thus removing the legal protection of their civilian passengers. Wilson refused to do this. Bryan had no choice but to resign as secretary of state. Not only would Wilson not protest to the British over arming merchant ships but he had permitted forbidden munitions to be shipped on the ocean liner, providing a second legal ground to allow the Germans to fire upon the *Lusitania*. As Bryan pointed out, "Germany has a right to prevent contraband from going to the Allies, and a ship carrying contraband should not rely upon passengers to protect her from attack—it would be like putting women and children in front of an army."[18]

One may differ with the reform and populist beliefs held by Bryan, but it must also be acknowledged that here was a man worthy of our respect. Bryan's Christian ethics and personal integrity would not allow him to countenance the lies President Wilson would have him publish in the name of the United States.

The Wilsonian influence did not end with his administration in early 1921. He had altered the American society too deeply for that. His tactics of intolerance in the name of idealism seduced an entire generation, and established a pattern of authoritarian socialism that endures to this day. Historians have described the Wilson administration as a watershed of change in political America.

Wilson's tactics even penetrated the United States Supreme Court, which upheld his peculiar ideas of patriotism that sacrificed the principles of free speech, a free press, and a voluntary army. After World War I the Supreme Court, previously wary of sweeping "reforms" in the name of the Constitution, became far less inhibited.

Although the administrations that immediately followed Wilson (specifically Harding and Coolidge) broke with Wilson's methods, most politicians in both major parties were deeply impressed with the success of Wilson's power drive. Today, both leading Republican and Democratic politicians hail Wilson as one of the greatest presidents. The Wilsonian attempt to force other nations and cultures to adopt the American pattern remains embedded in our foreign policy, as is the lofty Wilsonian rhetoric, the intolerance of contradiction, and the tendency to confuse liberalism with righteousness.

Presidents Richard Nixon and Ronald Reagan have both publicly expressed their admiration for Woodrow Wilson. And it is a law of human nature that we seek to imitate what we most admire.

The 1920s—Socialism Rejected

As we have seen, America and Europe parted company at the time of America's War for Independence and the European revolutions. America went the route of freedom, joining Europe in the practice of socialism and repression only during the Wilson era. After the war, America and Europe again parted company for what was to prove only a short period of years.

Post World War I Europe was a bitter, disillusioned place. The young men back from the front were war-weary and angry with their leaders who had kept them in the trenches for so long. Rather than demanding truly free governments, the people demanded more socialism and welfare handouts. In Britain, the 1920s saw the socialist Labour party form its first government. In Italy, the National Socialists or Fascists under Mussolini were brought to power.

Germany was especially in adverse circumstances. The Treaty of Versailles, ending the war, had forced Germany to agree to pay unreasonably large reparation payments to the Allies. These reparations had more to do with the Allies' lust for revenge and desire to keep Germany weak than it did with compensation for actual damage done. So bitter were the Allies toward Germany that on the excuse that Germany had defaulted on its payments, France and Belgium occupied the Ruhr on January 11, 1923. France delcared martial law in that area and cut post, telegraph, and telephone links with the outside world. It must be pointed out that Great Britain protested this action.

In the end, Germany tried to pay its debt by simply printing more money and causing hyperinflation. Its intention was to pay the reparations in virtually worthless currency. In 1913 the German mark was worth $2.38. By 1918 a mark was down to only 7¢. In the middle of 1922 1¢ would buy 100 marks. By the summer of 1923 a visiting congressman got 4,000 million marks for $7.00.[19]

On the other hand, the Americans had had enough of socialism and European-style repressive government. The American people had their chance on November 2, 1920, and they took it with a vengeance. In that presidential election, the Americans showed what they thought of Wilson and the Democratic Party by giving the Republican Party the greatest landslide victory in American history up to that time. Senator Warren Harding of Ohio, the Republican candidate, captured

16,152,200 or 61 percent of the vote as opposed to Governor James Cox, also of Ohio, who received 9,147,353 or 34.5 percent of the vote. As an ironic footnote, the next month, on December 10, Woodrow Wilson won the Nobel Peace Prize.[20]

It is sad to note that down through the years President Harding and his Vice President Calvin Coolidge have received a bad press. The first charge against Harding was that he packed his cabinet with his old cronies. In the first place, all presidents before and since have given their closest associates top government positions. Moreover, as historian Paul Johnson observed, "The cabinet list was a cross-section of successful America; a car manufacturer, two bankers, a hotel director, a farm-journal editor, an international lawyer, a rancher, an engineer and only two professional politicians."[21]

Speaking of the cabinet, it is interesting to note that Albert Fall, the main character in the Teapot Dome scandal that the Democrats tried to make political capital out of, was unanimously confirmed as interior secretary by the U. S. Senate, the only cabinet member in American history to be so honored.[22] As thirty-seven of the ninety-six senators were Democrats, these senators could not honestly criticize Harding for nominating Fall, since they all voted for his confirmation.

The Teapot Dome story, put briefly, involved the desire of the navy to take oil from their western oil leases and stockpile it at the navy installation at Pearl Harbor, Hawaii. The navy asked Secretary of the Interior Fall to handle this project. Fall reached an agreement with the Mammoth Oil Company and the Pan American Oil Company to perform this task. The terms of the contract were highly favorable to the oil companies. The Democrats in Congress, seeing an opportunity to embarrass the Republicans, undertook an investigation. They asked two questions: Why had Fall concluded a contract with these two firms without putting it out for bids, giving all the oil companies a chance at it? Their follow-up question was, had Fall received a bribe from Mammoth and Pan American? These investigations did little damage to the Republicans for two reasons: First of all, when the investigation took place Harding was dead and Coolidge was president. Second, Fall had already been removed from office by President Harding before his death.

There is no evidence that Harding did anything illegal as president. The Harding papers were opened to the inspection of historians in 1964. There was no trace of corruption to be found in Harding's conduct. However, attitudes were already fixed; conventional wisdom has Harding guilty of all sorts of sins. His memory will remain wrongly stained, probably to the end of time.[23]

The truth was that Harding set the nation on the road to prosperity by removing oppressive government interference with the rights of the citizens and cutting government spending. Under Harding, the government spend 40 percent less than it did under Wilson in peacetime. Harding took office in March 1921 in the midst of a deep recession; by July of the same year the economy was booming.[24] In four months an economic miracle had taken place, but Harding was destined never to receive the honor he so richly deserved.

With Harding's death in 1923, Calvin Coolidge became president. Coolidge generally is not highly regarded. While no accusation was ever made against his honesty, Coolidge is portrayed as a colorless, dry man who did little; not being talkative, he was nicknamed "Silent Cal." Part of this reputation is due to the man himself, who deliberately built up this image. The truth is that Coolidge was a very intelligent man with a dry sense of humor. Somehow his colorlessness made him colorful to the American public, who loved him. In 1924 he was reelected president in a landslide, capturing 54.1 percent of the vote to the Democrat's 28.8 percent; there were a large number of third-party candidates that year.

In truth Coolidge was a very able man who had climbed steadily in his political career. He went from parish councilor to assemblyman to mayor to state representative to state senator to lieutenant governor to governor to vice president. As governor of Massachusetts, he proved his ability by breaking the police strike of 1919. Coolidge called out the national guard, sacked the striking policemen, and hired new men to take their places. He had the courage to act decisively when necessary and won the admiration of the public for it.

The economy kept improving under Coolidge because he did not allow the government to interfere. As political humorist Will Rogers observed, "He didn't do anything, but that's what the people wanted done."[25] Indeed, Coolidge at points reminded one of the Puritans from his native New England. Coolidge echoed the Puritan emphasis on self-government when he addressed the Massachusetts Senate in 1914: "Government cannot relieve from toil. The normal must take care of themselves. Self-government means self-support."[26] Paul Johnson has called for a reappraisal of Harding and Coolidge.

While Harding and Coolidge were able to get America back on its feet economically, the rot had set in too deeply under Wilson to be destroyed. Two forces were at work which would ruin their work.

First of all, there was the conflict between the rural Christians and the urban intellectuals. Wilson's efforts to take what Christianity there was out of the state schools and replace it with statism had succeeded only too well. As the 1920s progressed, the generation that had been educated during the Wilson years came of age and entered society. This indoctrinated intellectual elite gained influence in American life, the media, and politics. This group was in direct conflict with the rural areas of America which still held to Christian values. The rural population looked at the intellectuals with distrust as being educated heathen; the intellectuals looked upon the country folk and their religion as old-fashioned superstition among the hicks and hayseeds.

These urban intellectuals in the news media censored any information which showed socialism in a bad light. One example which illustrates this is Stalin's drive to organize the Russian peasants into collective farms. Stalin did this ruthlessly, causing a great famine in the process. The American intellectuals maintained a news blackout on these events. Even when news of Stalin's ruthlessness seeped out, the socialist elite was not disturbed. After all, they argued, the Inquisition, in which people were tortured in order to eliminate heretics, did not discredit Christianity. Why should Stalin's purges be taken as a discredit to socialism? It was this generation of intellectuals which set up the "liberal establishment" which has controlled every administration from Franklin Roosevelt to the present.

The second cause of the collapse of the 1920s, one which led directly to the crash, was the expansion of credit. People went heavily into debt in order to purchase things on credit. This practice created masses of make-believe money which existed only on the pages of ledger books. Massive stock purchases on margin became commonplace.

When the stock market crashed in October of 1929, $3,000 million of stock value, make-believe money, disappeared .[27] Since these stocks were bought with borrowed money, figures added to bank accounts, the banks quickly demanded that those who borrowed money repay it. A chain reaction set in. Debtors could not repay banks, and banks could not repay depositors, having themselves lost in the crash. In many cases, the banks collapsed, as did businesses.

Although this was a tragedy for millions of people, in the long run the crash could have been healthy. At this time America was still on the gold standard; every dollar the government issued was backed by a dollar's worth of gold. The crash destroyed the make-believe ledger-account money. The smaller amount of real money then left was sound and, left to themselves, Americans could put their shattered economy back together.

This might have happened had Harding or Coolidge been president. However, in 1928 the nation elected another Republican president, Herbert Hoover. Hoover, a difficult man to classify, was in one sense the typical conservative Republican in the Harding/Coolidge mold. Curiously enough, there was another, rather surprising side to the president. Herbert Hoover had actually been a Republican member of the Wilson administration. Hoover had served first as chairman of the Commission for Relief in Belgium and then as chairman of the food administration. In this latter position, he assisted Wilson's government interference in the American economy. For instance, he fixed the price of wheat at two dollars a bushel and established a government grain corporation to buy and sell it. He supervised purchases of other foods as well and encouraged Americans to eat less and produce more.[28] He had a political philosophy closer to Wilson than to Harding and Coolidge.

Another colleague of his in the Wilson administration greatly admired him; he was Franklin Delano Roosevelt, assistant secretary of the navy. He commended Hoover, commenting, "He is certainly a wonder and I wish we could make him President of the United States. There could not be a better one."[29] This is ironic, considering that in 1932 the two men were to fight a bitter presidential campaign. Obviously, Roosevelt's political philosophy had not been offended by Hoover's performance during the Wilson years.

One of the effects of a depression, when the amount of money on the books shrinks, is that prices and wages fall. In an inflation, when the government prints all the money it wishes, prices go up, and so do wages. A depression is the exact opposite. With the make-believe money in the ledgers gone, there is less money; with less money around, prices and wages go down, because wages and prices are only finding their natural levels in proportion to the smaller amount of money to go around.

Unfortunately, the socialist side of Hoover's background came into play here. Wages were dropping, so he decided to take steps to keep them high. As a result of Hoover's efforts to keep wages high, the number of unemployed people rose dramatically.

Hoover had been warned not to do this. Andrew Mellon, his secretary of the treasury, advised him to keep the government's hands off the situation and let the laws of economics perform their natural healing process. This, Mellon said, would "purge the rottenness from the economy."[30]

Because unemployment was rising, Hoover had the government hire workers to labor on government projects; this is commonly referred to as "public works." Franklin Roosevelt gets credit for the public works he organized, but Hoover's record here was notable. As Johnson says, "More major public works were started in Hoover's four years than in the previous thirty, including the San Francisco Bay Bridge, the Los Angeles Aqueduct and the Hoover Dam...."[31]

Hoover also had the Federal Reserve make more money in credit. The credit collapse was to be cured by more credit! In the last week of October 1929 alone, he made $3000 million in new credit available.

The crash had caused the banks to demand that those who owed them money pay their loans. This caused massive bankruptcies and foreclosures. However, as Hoover saw thousands going bankrupt, he panicked and made it more difficult for banks to take action against those who owed them money. The banks, finding it increasingly difficult to recoup their losses, went bankrupt at a quicker rate than before. As Johnson comments:

His policy of public investment prevented necessary liquidations. The businesses he hoped thus to save either went bankrupt in the end, after fearful agonies, or were burdened throughout the 1930's by a crushing load of debt. Hoover undermined property rights by weakening the bankruptcy laws and encouraging states to halt auction-sales for debt, ban foreclosures or impose debt moratoria. This, in itself, impeded the ability of the banks to save themselves and maintain confidence. Hoover deliberately pushed federal credits into the banks and bullied them into inflating, thus increasing their precarious position.[32]

The Hoover disaster grew, as did unemployment under Roosevelt.

Franklin Roosevelt's New Deal

Franklin Roosevelt was not a man of original ideas. His greatest political mentor was Woodrow Wilson. As assistant secretary of the navy under Wilson, Roosevelt and other young men of that earlier administration learned that the American nation could be commanded from Washington, D. C.

The controls of President Wilson's wartime administration were largely temporary in nature, and were swept away by the succeeding Republican administration of Warren G. Harding. President Roosevelt determined that the controls of the New Deal would be permanent. In the specific measures he first proposed, however, President Roosevelt applied the tactics of President Hoover. It could be said that President Roosevelt was President Hoover—with teeth. (It should not be forgotten that Hoover also learned his political lessons as part of the Wilson administration.)

Hoover's bid for reelection was defeated more by the depression and the miseries it attached to his administration than to any campaign tactic of Roosevelt. Roosevelt was aware of this and campaigned on a platform of conservative promises and masterful evasions of delicate issues.

One example of Roosevelt's evasiveness during the campaign involved the gold standard. Hoover had claimed that if Roosevelt was elected president he would take America's dollar off the gold standard. Senator Glass, a Democrat, spoke in the Senate in defense of candidate Roosevelt. He said, "With nearly 40 percent of the gold supplies in the world, why are we going off the gold standard? The suggestion that we may devalue the gold dollar 50 percent means national repudiation. It means dishonor. It is immoral."[33] In short, Glass denied that Roosevelt had any intention of doing this. FDR supported Glass: "Senator Glass made a devastating challenge that no responsible government would have sold to the country securities payable in gold if it knew that the promise—yes, the covenant embodied in these securities—was as dubious as the President of the United States claims it was."[34]

One of the first things Roosevelt did, shortly after becoming president, was to take America off the gold standard. Glass was horrified and publicly apologized to Hoover in a speech in the Senate. He was to have been FDR's secretary of the treasury, but he refused the position after this breach of faith.

As soon as Roosevelt became president, he ordered all banks to be closed until he could order a large quantity of money printed for them to give to those who wished to withdraw their accounts. Then he sent a bill to Congress to make what he had already done legal; at the time he closed the banks, he had no legal power to do so. The bill he sent to Congress also required the banks to get a government license to re-open. Furthermore, it ordered Americans to turn their uncoined gold in to the government in exchange for newly printed paper money. Thus did the American economy and banking system come under total government control from that time into the present.

During the famous first hundred days of Roosevelt's New Deal, Congress passed the president's bills fast and furiously. It took years before many people realized to what extent the New Deal transformed America from a more or less free country into a somewhat national socialist state.

The Roosevelt dollar stopped the money supply from shrinking and caused it to expand rapidly. Roosevelt had to be sure that the money circulated; prices had to stop falling and begin to rise. The actual price of goods would go up as the amount of money circulating went up, the reason being that each dollar would then purchase less goods. The new money had to reach the farmers quickly in order to stop them from defaulting on the mortgages and going bankrupt. FDR encouraged the rise of farm-produce prices by paying the farmers to produce less food. The shrinking of the supply of farm produce on the market would be another pressure forcing prices up. This, in turn, meant that the farmers would have the paper money to pay off their loans. This practice also applied to manufacturing and the trades. The administration set up the Office of Price Administration, in which government price fixing was called "fair trading." Industry was not being regulated to keep prices from falling; it was agreeing to "codes."[35]

Those who did not accede to these regulations were in trouble. Witness one Jersey City tailor. He was caught pressing a pair of trousers for five cents less than the price set by the government. He was taken to court, fined, and put in prison.[36]

With such dictatorial regulations, it was only a matter of time until the president ran afoul of the Supreme Court. The Court began ruling that Roosevelt's programs were unconstitutional. His practice of dictating the prices businessmen could charge was one measure thrown out by the court. Roosevelt countered by introducing a bill in Congress which was a direct attack on the conservative majority of the court. Noting that several of the nine justices were old men, he proposed that if any justice aged seventy refused to retire on full pay, an additional justice would be named to the court. It was obvious what Roosevelt wanted: to pack the court with justices of his own choosing in order to gain its compliance. Even the Democratic members of Congress were offended by this scheme; they told FDR they would not support that bill. This threat, however, had the desired effect on the Supreme Court. From that time on the justices were more lenient with the New Deal legislation passed by the Congress. The New Deal steamroller had its way.

Garet Garrett gave an eloquent summary of the New Deal. He wrote:

In all these New Deal laws there was infringement of the individual's liberty. The employer was no longer free to hire and fire whom he would, nor to buy labor below a certain price; neither side to the labor contract was free. An American boy, with a tear in his eye and adventure in his heart, was no longer free to steal away over the kitchen roof at night and go forth to meet the world; there was no work for him in the world out there because the law said he was child labor and any employer who hired him would be forbidden access to the channels of interstate commerce. The wage earner had to have a union card and a Social Security number. The farmer was no longer free to do what he would with his own ground or his own wheat. No wage earner was any longer free to be so improvident as to consume the whole of his own earnings and forget his old age.

To enforce these laws it was necessary to create new agencies of government. Each new agency issued its own rules and regulations, having the force of law; and in a little while these administrative agencies were passing ten times as many laws as Congress, all binding on the people.[37]

Christians believe that God is their King. It is to God that they are duty-bound to look for direction in how to live their lives. It is to God they must look to provide them with the things they need to live. It is God who gives Christians direction and provides for their needs. The New Deal, on the other hand, was an attempt on the part of the State to try to take God's place in the lives of its citizens.

A key point of federal doctrine became federal sovereignty or lordship. The concern of Washington, people were told, was the public good, but this public good was seen in humanistic and statist, not biblical, terms. Men began to see their hope of salvation in political terms, and candidates began to run on platforms promising to "save" the country. Both political parties offered a political solution to man's problems, and all too many churches agreed. The social gospel is, after

149

all, a political gospel of salvation. Instead of healing and saving the people, this messianic plan of statist salvation created national and international problems. One writer, after World War II, raised a pertinent question in a book on the subject, *Will dollars save the world?* It was soon evident that neither dollars nor politics could save the world, as conditions in the post-World War II era saw the increase of wars, crime, mass murders, racial hostility, and more. Politics had become the pseudolight that failed.

Chapter 8 Notes

1. David Tyack and Elizabeth Hansot, *Managers of Virtue* (New York: Basic Books, 1983), p. 19.
2. Otto Scott, *Robespierre, the Voice of Virtue* (New York: Mason & Lipscomb, 1974), p. 73.
3. Ibid., p. 96.
4. Otto Scott, *The Professional* (New York: Atheneum Publishers, 1976), pp. 39, 8ff.
5. Colin Simpson, *The Lusitania* (Boston: Little, Brown, 1972), p. 27.
6. Ibid., pp. 157–158.
7. Antony Sutton, *Wall Street and the Rise of Hitler* (Seal Beach, California: '76 Press, 1976), p. 175.
8. Paul Johnson, *Modern Times* (New York: Harper & Row, 1983), p. 66.
9. Ibid., p. 204.
10. Antony Sutton, *Wall Street and the Bolshevik Revolution* (New Rochelle, New York: Arlington House, 1974), p. 46.
11. David M. Kennedy, *Over Here: The First World War and American Society* (New York: Oxford University Press, 1980), pp. 87–88.
12. Ibid.
13. Johnson, *Modern Times*, p. 206.
14. Ibid., p. 206.
15. Richard L. Perry, *Sources of Our Liberties* (Chicago: American Bar Foundation, 1959), p. 411.
16. Samuel Eliot Morison and Henry Steele Commager, *The Growth of the American Republic* (New York: Oxford University Press, revised edition, 1960), vol. 2, pp. 478–479.

17. Ibid., vol. 2, pp. 457–458.
18. Johnson, *Modern Times*, pp. 134–135.
19. Morison and Commager, *American Republic*, p. 904.
20. Calvin D. Linton, ed., *The American Almanac* (Nashville: Thomas Nelson Publishers, 1975, revised 1977), pp. 300–301.
21. Johnson, *Modern Times*, p. 216.
22. Ibid., pp. 215–216.
23. Ibid., pp. 218–219.
24. Ibid., p. 216.
25. Ibid., p. 220.
26. Ibid., p. 221.
27. Frederick Lewis Allen, *The Big Change* (New York: Harper & Bros., 1952), p. 145.
28. Morison and Commager, *American Republic*, pp. 471–472.
29. Johnson, *Modern Times*, p. 242.
30. Ibid., p. 244.
31. Ibid., p. 246.
32. Garet Garrett, *The American Story* (Chicago: Regnery, 1955), pp. 261–262.
33. Ibid., p. 249.
34. Scott, *Professional*, p. 171.
35. Garrett, *American Story*, p. 274.
36. Ibid., p. 281.

The Unfinished Story

NINE

As we have seen, Europe and America went their separate ways after World War I. America revolted against the wartime socialism and loss of freedom imposed by President Wilson and returned to the free society to which it was accustomed. In Europe it was far different. These nations across the Atlantic continued their socialistic policies. Not only were their policies socialistic but there was a sinister, warlike element to them as well.

Under Lenin, the Soviet Union adapted a "command system of government" under which the nation took its orders from the central government without a chance to vote or even debate Lenin's policies. Lenin also had the nation on a war economy. This meant that the first priority of the nation's industry and agriculture was to support the development of the armed forces and prepare for war. Consumer goods for the civilian market consisted of whatever was left after the military needs were met. This was not a normal policy for a nation in peacetime.

When Fascist dictator Benito Mussolini came to power in Italy in November 1922, he, too, curbed personal freedom and established the command system of government. In this effort, he systematically eliminated those groups opposed to his rule. Although it was obvious that Mussolini was no friend of freedom, he continued to be courted by all the other major countries of Europe.

On January 30, 1933, Adolf Hitler became chancellor of Germany. The post of chancellor is the equivalent of that of prime minister in Great Britain and Canada. Hitler quickly took dictatorial power over the nation, destroying his opposition and establishing the command system of government. He also put the German economy on a war footing. As the European nations began to destroy the liberties of the people and to prepare for war, only idealists who refused to face facts believed that the world was on the verge of what British Prime Minister Neville Chamberlain called "peace in our time."

In point of fact, Great Britain at the start of the Second World War presented a strange and sad political state of affairs. At this time, the conservatives held a majority in the House of Commons against the socialist Labour party. Chamberlain, his policies defeated and his health failing (he died on November 9, 1940), resigned the premiership to be succeeded by Winston Churchill on May 10, 1940. Although the conservatives were strong enough in the House of Commons to form a government with Labour in opposition, this was not done; the nation was at war and it was believed that Britain would be better served by a government of both major parties united, a coalition government. To combine conservatives and socialists is like combining oil and water, which do not mix. Although Prime Minister Churchill was a conservative, many influential ministers were socialists. These men of the Labour party soon took control of the United Kingdom's bureaucracy. During the war, the socialist leaders of the Labour party indoctrinated the troops, influencing them toward socialism.

In one move toward a less democratic government, elections were suspended until after the war. By then, the strength of socialist influence was felt as Churchill, wartime leader and hero, was defeated in a landslide by Labour.

How the War Affected Britain

With the fall of France to the Germans in mid-1940 and America not yet in the war, Great Britain stood alone against the vast German war machine. The British, quickly realizing they did not have the resources to defeat the Germans, appealed to the neutral United States for assistance in supplying arms and supplies. President Roosevelt was ready to help. The result was a deal called Lend-Lease. President Roosevelt agreed to give Britain fifty overage destroyers in exchange for two concessions. First of all, Great Britain was forced to sell all of her financial holdings in the United States at bargain-basement prices. Second, Britain had to allow the United States Navy to establish bases on British territory in the Western Hemisphere. The bases thus leased to the Americans included Georgetown, British Guiana, Trinidad, Saint Lucia, Antigua, Jamaica, Bermuda, and Newfoundland.

When the Lend-Lease Bill came before the Congress, the legislators were very disturbed. They felt that supplying arms to Great Britain in this way was a violation of the United States' role as a neutral power. Not least among the congressional protesters were Democrats, men of President Roosevelt's own party. Representative Hugh Peterson, Democrat of Georgia, stated, "This is no defensive measure. It is a measure of aggressive warfare....This legislation, cloaked in the robes of peace, is in its naked form a cowardly declaration of war."[1] Senator Bennett Clark, Democrat of Missouri, added, "This is not a defense bill, it is a war bill. We pledge ourselves to assuring guaranteeing military victory of one belligerent over another."[2] Testifying before a congressional committee, Secretary of the Navy Frank Knox was pressed into a corner by the legislators. He was forced to admit that convoying ships carrying American military aid across the Atlantic Ocean was "an act of war."[3]

According to British historian Paul Johnson, both the Americans and the British had ulterior motives. He writes, "...in return for the agreement [Britain] virtually surrendered the remains of her export trade to the United States and...undertook to abandon Imperial Preference after the war, which for Cordell Hull [U.S. secretary of state] had been throughout a more important foreign policy aim than the containment of totalitarian power....Lend-Lease was important to Churchill simply because he believed it might tempt Hitler into conflict with the United States."[4]

One thing is certain; with the passing of Lend-Lease by Congress, America did compromise her neutrality. One of the more blatant violations of neutrality involved taking possession of all German and Italian ships then in United States ports.[5]

Indeed, the American people did not want a war. In the autumn of 1935, when pollsters asked the American people whether Congress should get a national vote before declaring a war, 75 percent of those questioned said yes.[6]

In January 1937, the Gallup organization asked, "Do you think it was a mistake for the United States to enter the [first] World War?" Seventy percent said yes, it was a mistake.[7] These were not the attitudes of a people thirsting for war.

In fact, in 1940, when Europe was at war, the Democratic party platform for the presidential election stated: "We will not participate in foreign wars, and we will not send our army, naval, or air forces to fight in foreign lands outside of the Americas, except in case of attack....The direction and aim of our foreign policy has been, and will continue to be, the security and defense of our own land and the maintenance of its peace."[8] That statement, a bit wordy, is in effect Roosevelt's equivalent to President Wilson's successful 1916 campaign slogan, "He kept us out of war."

Perhaps a more accurate assessment of Roosevelt's feelings about fighting a war can be found in this footnote from James Thomas's book *Holy War*: "While still a President-elect [November 1932-March 1933] FDR told Rexford Tugwell that war with Japan might as well come now as later. Shortly thereafter FDR allocated National Recovery funds for warship construction."[9]

One of the segments of American society, but by no means the only one, which opposed our getting involved in the Second World War was the left-wing Communist sympathizers. After Hitler invaded the Soviet Union, their attitude changed. From that time on, they were anxious for America to become involved. Up to this time, another group of Americans anxious not to become involved was the America First movement. However, after the invasion of the Soviet Union, forces were set to work to destroy their public image. America First was made to look like a Fascist organization, one small example among many showing the power of the media to sway the public awareness of millions.

Had America simply joined the United Kingdom in fighting Germany, one could have made a case for saying that the free nations of the world were fighting against dictatorships.

Churchill and Roosevelt were willing to join hands with any nation that would join them in fighting Hitler, regardless of its moral character. Churchill was quite straightforward about this when he said, "If Hitler invaded Hell, I would at least make a favorable reference to the Devil...."[10]

Britain and America seemed quite willing to forget that the Soviet Union had been Germany's partner in the invasion of Poland, the act that had triggered the war. The Soviets' behavior was at least as inhumane as that of Hitler's forces. In the spring of 1940, the Soviets killed fifteen thousand Polish officers, possibly at the suggestion of Hitler's Gestapo. In fact, Stalin's secret police, the KGB, worked closely with the Gestapo right up until Germany's invasion of the Soviet Union on June 22, 1941. The KGB had, for instance, handed over several hundred Germans, mainly Communists and Jews, to the Gestapo.[11] These things were quietly forgotten. Nor did Stalin's behavior improve once he joined the West against Germany. Political prisoners held in those areas of the USSR open to German attack were massacred.[12]

In order to defeat the Germans, Churchill was quite prepared to resort to total war by attacking civilian targets in terror raids. Writing to Lord Beaverbrook, Churchill stated:

> When I look round to see how we can win the war I see that there is only one sure path. We have no Continental army which can defeat the German military power. The blockade is broken and Hitler has Asia and probably Africa to draw from. Should he be repulsed here or not try invasion, he will recoil eastward, and we have nothing to stop him. But there is one thing that will bring him back and bring him down, and that is an absolutely devastating, exterminating attack by very heavy bombers from this country upon the Nazi homeland.[13]

America Goes to War

Had Japan not attacked Pearl Harbor on December 7, 1941, President Roosevelt probably would not have been able to get Congress to declare war on Japan. Likewise, had Germany not committed the blunder of declaring war upon the United States at this time, Congress might not have declared war on that nation either. Both nations made the error of making enemies of more of the world than they could cope with. Greed was their undoing.

Until America's entry into the war, the struggle was waged to stop Hitler's expansion of his territory by invasion and to liberate those nations under his control. This was a practical goal. The Soviet Union, however, described the war objective as the creation of a better world. This was a humanistic objective. Its argument is that mankind and the State comprise the one true god, not Jehovah, the God of the Bible.

The Bible promises a time when Christianity shall have won its battle with evil, a time when God's people shall rule the world in peace by the power of the Holy Spirit. This prospect, as we have seen in earlier chapters, is referred to as the millennium. What the Allies were trying to do was to set up a millennium without God. They themselves would play God; they would set up a perfect world. That their godlike plans were opposed to the Bible came over only too strongly when one viewed their willingness to join forces with evil despots like Stalin and to use immoral methods such as the terror bombing of civilians.

With the entry of America into the war, Roosevelt took the same steps that Wilson did before him. He put America on a war economy and transformed the American republic into a nation with a command system of government. This involved measures which included the censorship of the press.

One interesting measure of repression was the Smith Act. This act was quite similar to the Sedition Act of 1918. Its purpose was to restrict the right of the people to publicly disagree with the government. The interesting feature of this act was that in practice it was only used to suppress American Trotskyite Communists. This would have pleased Stalin very much. Communism had within it two strains of thought, that held by the Trotskyites and that held by the Stalinists; one could compare this with the Christian religion, which has within it various denominations. The Stalinists were very anxious to suppress the Trotskyites, to the point of having Trotsky murdered in Mexico. In effect, America's government took Stalin's part in an internal Communist struggle.

This war to create a better world ended on the same amoral note on which it was fought. The Western Allies forced at least 2 million Russian refugees, some of whom had fled Russia during the 1917 Bolshevik Revolution, back to the Soviet Union and certain death.[14]

One side effect of the war was the raising of educational standards in the United States. The war effort had required a work force with various skills. The government paid to have its citizens, civilian and military, learn the trades that were needed. This training had positive and negative aspects. On the positive side, America became better skilled and educated. The benefits of creating a high-quality labor pool would transform American industry both during and after the war into one of the best in the world. Another benefit was that, under the G.I. Bill, the government paid for the veterans of the war to go to colleges and universities. Thus higher education, once the province of the elite, became a mass movement. On the other hand, American life became more institutionalized. Formal education became the means by which Americans improved their status. A largely theoretical university education replaced practical apprenticeship as the means of entering business or the trades.

As a general observation, it is also true that Americans became accustomed to the government arranging their lives for them. This continues.

After the First World War, a group of nations formed the League of Nations to protect the humanistic "millennium" of peace and goodwill. Like all attempts to play God, it failed. World War II proved how powerless the league was. After the second global conflict, the nations of the world showed how much they had learned from history by creating a new league called the United Nations.

The United Nations quickly proved that it could not keep the peace any better than the old League of Nations could. The Communists expanded their forces into the Korean peninsula in Asia, thus creating another crisis. President Truman was authorized by the United Nations to organize resistance to the Communist North. The United States never declared war on either North Korea or China. Technically America was not at war; Korea was a "police action." Because there was no war, the media were able to criticize without restraint, which they did.

Another aspect of this war which was not a war was that America was not striving to win. James Thomas summed up the explanation given by one high government official this way: "...the object would not be the punishment or even the destruction of the North Koreans. All we ought to do, he said, 'is see that the [North Korean] attack failed.' "[15] The two sides had different aims in that war. The North Koreans wanted to win. The Americans simply wanted to stop the Communist attack.

Another area in which postwar America occupied itself was in the area of equal rights. The government felt that the time had come to halt the discrimination against the Negro population of America and ensure that all citizens were treated equally. As with other issues, the federal government had only limited authority under the Constitution over the lives and individual practices of the citizens. The equal-rights measures did some good and some evil. Their major result was an increase of federal power.

The movement for equality then evolved into something different. The whole situation followed the pattern of the antislavery movement of the previous century. At that time, moderates were looking for a way to stop the practice of slavery. Out of that movement came men who had confused the Christian religion with the antislavery cause. With evangelistic zeal they demanded immediate abolition, by force if need be. In the same way, liberal churchmen, having rejected the Christian Gospel, found a new gospel in what became the civil-rights movement, world peace, abortion, "gay rights," and more. Modernism was taking the initiative while evangelical churches were mainly reacting.

The difficulty with the civil-rights campaign was in the visionary zeal with which its proponents tried, in a very brief period of time, to change the attitudes and practices developed over generations. Whereas the early equality movement might have irritated and annoyed some of the citizens, the radical civil-rights movement created real feelings of fear and intimidation.

One milestone along the civil-rights path was the Civil Rights Act of 1964, signed by President Johnson. He attempted to force Caucasian Americans to treat the Negroes as equals, not by persuasion but by government decree.

Hand in hand with Johnson's civil-rights efforts was his "war on poverty." This was a welfare program by which Johnson intended to do away with poverty by giving away government money. Jesus had said, "The poor you have with you always" (John 12:8 NKJV), but President Johnson hoped to change all that. He didn't.

Johnson had two wars going at the same time, and both cost money. At the same time he fought poverty at home, he was fighting Communist North Vietnam in Asia. Early in 1968, Johnson wanted to send the additional 206,000 troops the American commander in Vietnam had requested. However, his treasury secretary, Henry Fowler, objected. There wasn't enough money. If Johnson wanted to send the troops, fine, but his social programs would have to be cut back. In the words of historian Paul Johnson, "It was a significant turning point in American history; the first time the Great Republic, the richest nation on earth, came up against the limits of its financial resources."[16] Johnson wanted to have his cake and eat it, too. What the president did was to take America deeper and deeper into debt, borrowing money and spending it. As we have seen previously, a government that expands the amount of money in circulation—either by printing more or by credit—creates inflation. This was the result of Johnson's policies. Inflation was to become so serious that President Nixon was to impose wage/price controls for the first time in American history in time of peace. Incidentally, this didn't solve the inflation problem. The classic result of wage/price controls is shortages. These began to appear during the Nixon controls. The controls were not in place long enough for the shortages to become widely noticed.

Vietnam

Vietnam was in reality another Korea, but without United Nations involvement. It was a "police action," initiated by Presidents Kennedy and Johnson. Once again, the United States never played the game to win. Henry Cabot Lodge, the American ambassador to South Vietnam, told President Johnson, "In truth, we do not need to define 'victory' and then go ahead and achieve it one hundred percent." All America needed was a "psychological victory."[17] Unfortunately, the North Vietnamese defined victory in only one way: winning the war.

One might not approve of press censorship as practiced in World War II, but in Vietnam we saw the other extreme. For instance, when American forces made a daring raid into North Vietnam to rescue prisoners of war, the press was critical. The raid was denounced as "provocative" and compared with a John Wayne movie.[18]

In January 1968, the North launched its famous Tet Offensive in which Communist forces swept the South. The American media hailed this as a great American defeat. The opposite was true. The northern forces had two aims. First of all, they wished to win a great tactical success which would place them in a command position. Second, they wanted to spark off a mass uprising against the South Vietnamese government; they were certain the sympathies of the peasants must be with them. The Tet Offensive failed. The North suffered heavy losses and came out of the offensive with a weaker army. There was no tactical success and no uprising. Yet the media portrayed this as a victory for the North and a defeat for the United States. This incident was crucial in the process of disillusionment with the war.[19]

In this climate created by the media and sustained by the American government's refusal to try to win a victory, President Nixon had to secure United States withdrawal from Vietnam. A compromise peace was negotiated. After the American government was weakened by the Watergate episode, North Vietnam broke the agreement and took over the whole country.

President Nixon also adopted the strategy of foreign affairs which had been prevalent in Europe for so long, that of balancing one power off against another. This policy had not worked in Europe, as we see from their long history of wars, and it was not destined to work for the Americans. Still, with great optimism Nixon spoke of this concept, even to the point of implying that a strong Soviet Union and Red China were beneficial. In 1972 he stated:

> We must remember the only time in the history of the world that we have had any extended periods of peace is when there has been balance of power. It is when one nation becomes infinitely more powerful in relation to its potential competitor that the danger of war arises. So I believe in a world in which the United States is powerful. I think it will be a safer world and a better world if we have a strong, healthy United States, Europe, Soviet Union, China, Japan, each balancing the other, not playing one against the other, an even balance.[20]

It was in the spirit of this philosophy that Nixon conducted his foreign policy. He continued the process of détente with Red China and the Soviet Union, thus obscuring the moral superiority of free countries over dictatorships. His foreign policy was not based on moral principle but on what would give America (he thought) practical advantages in the international community.

There was no mistaking America's choice for president in 1972, however. Pitted against Democratic Senator George McGovern, a radical liberal who made no effort to hide it, Nixon won one of the largest landslide victories in American history. He received 47,169,911 votes (61.8 percent) to McGovern's 29,170,383 (38.2 percent).[21]

The media and President Nixon had long been at odds with each other. However, although Nixon disliked it, he gave the media credit for having more power than it actually had. He told his staff, "Remember, the press is the enemy. When news is concerned, nobody in the press is a friend. They are all enemies."[22] Although every indication pointed to his massive landslide against McGovern, Nixon "ran scared." He constantly overrated the strength of his opponents. The results of the atmosphere which he created around him was a clumsy break-in at the Democratic party headquarters in Washington's Watergate complex.

The media smelled blood. Although they were not able to prevent Nixon's reelection, they were out to discredit him. Watergate was their tool, and they used it viciously. The media went about the destruction of the president of the United States with a brutal efficiency. Their first objective was to destroy Vice President Spiro T. Agnew. Agnew went around the country denouncing the press, saying out loud all the things Nixon felt in his heart. It would never do to hound Nixon out of office only to be faced with a President Agnew. Going back into Agnew's record as governor of Maryland, a post he had resigned four years earlier to become vice president, the press unearthed evidence that he had taken bribes at that time. Agnew pleaded no contest when the charge came to court. Nixon appointed the minority leader of the U.S. House of Representatives, Gerald Ford, to take Agnew's place.

After a series of convictions of White House aides and a couple of cabinet ministers, the guns of the media were aimed straight at the president. Although the courts had not allowed Senator Joseph Mc-Carthy to subpoena President Eisenhower's records for his committee hearings into Communist infiltration into the government, the judiciary was now more cooperative. White House tapes were subpoenaed by the Senate "Watergate Committee." First Judge John Sirica of the U.S. District Court ruled that the committee must have the tapes.

Impeachment loomed. As a result, on August 9, 1974, Richard Nixon became the first American president to resign his position. The president who had won the largest election landslide in American history was also the first to be forced from office. The media had actually been able to overturn the result of a presidential election.

Gerald Ford then became America's first unelected president. One of his first acts was to pardon Richard Nixon for any crimes he might have committed as president. This action, mightily criticized at the time, spared the nation the trauma of seeing a former president humiliated and possibly imprisoned.

When Gerald Ford appointed Nelson Rockefeller, former governor of New York, as vice president, he performed a first in American history. For the first time, neither president nor vice president had been elected by the American people in a general election. This was not the only first. Since the Congress, which had to confirm the nominations of both men as vice president, was controlled by Democrats, it was the first time that Democratic legislators had, in effect, voted into office a Republican president and vice president.

In 1976, Gerald Ford was renominated as the Republican presidential candidate, after winning a close, bruising battle with former Governor

Ronald Reagan of California. Due to pressure from conservative Republicans, Vice President Rockefeller was dropped from the ticket, with Senator Robert Dole becoming the vice presidential candidate. The Democrats nominated former Governor James "Jimmy" Carter of Georgia and Senator Walter Mondale of Minnesota. In a very close election, Carter led the Democrats to victory.

President Carter deserves some credit for raising the human-rights issue in foreign policy. By so doing, he struck the first note of morality in America's relations with the rest of the world in a long, long time. Unfortunately, Carter seemed more eager to apply his moral yardstick to America's friends rather than its enemies. This meant, in the end, that the Carter administration's concern on the moral issue of human rights was superficial.

The West grew uneasy about the trustworthiness of the U.S. under Carter. Carter's policy helped cause the downfall of friendly governments in Nicaragua and Iran. Relations with some Latin American countries grew strained. Brazil, for instance, canceled its defense pacts with the United States in September 1977. Argentina also lost interest in close cooperation with America.[23]

On the other hand, when the Soviet Union invaded Afghanistan, Carter cut off grain sales to the USSR and pressured the United States Olympic Team into withdrawing from competition in the 1980 Summer Olympic Games in Moscow.

The government's pressure upon America's churches increased under both Presidents Carter and Reagan. While the main-line denominations, which more or less automatically approved of the government's prosocialist policies at home and abroad, were not bothered very much, fundamentalists began to feel coercion from the government. Christians, tired of humanist state schools, had been withdrawing their children in increasing numbers from public schools for many years and starting their own schools. The State started to move quickly to bring both parents and Christian schools to court in virtually every state of the union. At the same time, in the name of the separation of Church and State, courts started to ban any religious element in public celebrations. The practice of invocations at high-school graduation ceremonies began to be challenged more and more. In 1982 President Reagan signed into law a bill which will force the churches to start paying social-security taxes starting in 1984, a move which extends the State's control of terms of employment between the Church (the representative of Christ the King here on earth) and its staff.

In 1983 Bob Jones University, a fundamentalist Christian college, lost its tax-exempt status because it refused to allow Negroes and whites to date one another. The reason given was that it was against "public policy." Churches and religious institutions can now only have tax-exempt status if what they preach and practice is in accordance with "public policy." But public policy is in favor of equal rights for women, thereby placing in jeopardy the Roman Catholic Church and the fundamentalist denominations which refuse to ordain women. Public policy is against discrimination toward homosexuals. Those Christians who believe with the Bible that homosexuals are sinful perverts are thus in trouble. Christians who preach that abortion is murdering babies are also facing threats. Public policy says that abortion is not murder. Christians who have picketed abortion clinics have been sued for slander by these clinical killers.

This is our predicament now, very similar to the conditions of nonconforming Christians in England during the reign of Charles I in the early seventeenth century. The State then and now has felt that all areas of life ought to be under its control.

Charles I and the U.S. federal government have both taxed heavily. The purpose of taxes is partly to gain funds, but taxation is a form of revolution in the modern age. Taxation is also used to control behavior. In order for churches and religious institutions to maintain their rightful tax exemptions, they must follow the guidelines laid down by the government.

This was also true in the days of Charles I. Only those belonging to the State church had "liberty." To belong to the State church meant, especially for ministers, that they had to approve of certain doctrines and practices in Church and State. The alternative was to be cast out, to become a nonconformist, and to be persecuted.

Some Christians, not willing to compromise, were driven to the point of leaving their native England. They came to America in search of religious freedom. Christians have now gone full circle. The conditions of the England of Charles I have found their way across the ocean to the land which sheltered those English religious outcasts, the United States of America, 1984.

There is, however, a difference. The Puritans of the seventeenth century were seeking to control a State church with their perspective. The embattled Christians of twentieth-century America seek to avoid controls on themselves and others: they want freedom for Christ's kingdom from the power of the State. Some centuries before the Puritans, John Wycliffe had begun a movement to place the Bible in the hands of the people. The survivors of his movement, the Lollards, merged with the Puritans. Step by step, the Christian society in the United States moved from the old-established-Church pattern to an emphasis on the separation of Church and State (*not* Christianity and the State) *and* a grass-roots faith; conversion, not State controls.

With the beginnings of the shift, hostilities toward the old Puritan orthodoxy began to appear. After 1815, Unitarianism became an openly avowed faith. One of its main fathers was an English philosopher of an earlier generation, John Locke. Locke set forth the basic premises of modernism, namely, that the philosophical (and scientific) thought of an age should determine the approach of men to the Bible. Locke was also a forefather of John Dewey and progressive education, with his insistence on the neutrality of the child's nature. Instead of being a sinner by his membership in Adam, for Locke the child's mind was a tabula rasa, a blank tablet for the educator to mold. Behaviorism, progressive education, John Dewey, Watson, and Skinner were intellectual heirs of Locke, and modernist pastors his religious heirs.

As against this, the "Bible only" foundation for faith arose in the United States to create a growing countermovement. In the late 1970s, liberal America was shocked to learn that over 50 million adult Americans described themselves as "born-again Christians." At the same time, these Christians were establishing the largest and fastest-growing churches in the United States. They were establishing Christian schools, more than six every day, homes for delinquent children, ministries to the needy, to prisoners, the sick, the aged, and others. The total gifts to such Christian ministries add up to a vast sum and indicate that Christ's kingdom is a growing, expanding power. The political order, rife with corruption, is increasingly suspect on all sides, while Christ's kingdom is gaining in power and recruits.

America is an unfinished story. As a result, it is sometimes a confused and stormy one. The fact remains that the United States, which began as a new experiment in civil order, continues to be such. The issues are now sharply drawn, more so than in 1776, between a top-down civil government and Church and a grass-roots faith which reorders Church and State from below.

Significantly, the modernist churches are losing members and are becoming "old folks' homes" of aging liberals. They have prestige in the media but not power with the Lord.

Important, too, in this present scene is another remarkable phenomenon, the charismatic movement. Without agreeing or disagreeing with its tenets, it must be noted that it is a major force among Protestants and Catholics. Moreover, one aspect of the charismatic movement is *not* new—the fact that it is grass-roots religion. The Holy Spirit works through persons, not institutions and bureaucracies. The old pattern saw Church and State as necessarily working through bureaucracies and official channels only. Under Tudor and Stuart monarchs, family worship was subject to suspicion and also arrest as a violation of the prerogatives of the State church. Now, among charismatic and noncharismatic alike, the power of God is seen as operating essentially in the believer.

This means a new doctrine of Christian power and social power, new in terms of Europe's history, but old in terms of Scripture.

The Puritans and others began as did their colonies, with their churches set forth earnestly and sincerely as the established Church. Gradually that pattern receded. Its disappearance has not meant the failure of the United States to be Christian. Rather, a separation took place. The State, step by step, followed the Unitarian and then the open humanistic pattern. The Church began to rebuild itself from the ground up.

The history of the Church since the beginning of the revivals of the nineteenth century is a checkered one. The revivals had their strengths and weaknesses. Many of the revivalists and camp-meeting preachers were ignorant men. Doctrine was sometimes weak or faulty, experience overstressed, and knowledge of Scripture neglected. Step by step, this grass-roots Christianity began to grow up, stress education, doctrine, Bible colleges, universities, Christian schools, and more, without losing but rather developing its faith.

Its liberal critics like to ridicule it as red-neck religion without knowing anything more about it than that they dislike and fear it. Such media abuse does not alter the facts of the rising power of biblical faith. The simple fact is that, day by day, the power base of the old order is being converted out from under it! The words of Paul to the Corinthians are finding a new fulfillment: "For ye see your calling, brethren, how that not many wise men after the flesh, not many mighty, not many noble, are called: But God hath chosen the foolish things of the world to confound the wise; and God hath chosen the weak things of the world to confound the things which are mighty" (1 Corinthians 1:26-27 KJV). The future of the United States as a Christian country will be written in terms of this fact.

Chapter 9 Notes

1. Charles A. Beard, *President Roosevelt and the Coming of the War 1941* (New Haven: Yale University Press, 1948), pp. 57–58.
2. Ibid., p. 63.
3. Ibid., p. 70.
4. Paul Johnson, *Modern Times* (New York: Harper & Row, 1983), p. 371.
5. Garet Garrett, *The American Story* (Chicago: Regnery, 1955), p. 310.
6. Frederick Lewis Allen, *The Big Change* (New York: Harper & Bros., 1952), p. 159.
7. Gallup Poll, 1937.
8. Beard, *Coming of the War*, p. 3.
9. James A. Thomas, *Holy War* (New Rochelle, New York: Arlington House, 1973), p. 27 footnote.
10. Otto Scott, *The Professional* (New York: Atheneum Publishers, 1976), p. 258.
11. Johnson, *Modern Times*, p. 373.
12. Ibid., p. 384.
13. Ibid., p. 370.
14. Scott, *Professional*, p. 303.
15. Thomas, *Holy War*, p. 189.
16. Johnson, *Modern Times*, p. 638.
17. Thomas, *Holy War*, p. 73.
18. Scott, *Professional*, p. 473.
19. Johnson, *Modern Times*, pp. 637–638.
20. Raymond Aron, *The Imperial Republic* (Lanham, Maryland: University Press of America, 1982).
21. Calvin D. Linton, ed., *American Almanac* (Nashville: Thomas Nelson Publishers, 1975, revised 1977), p. 420.
22. Johnson, *Modern Times*, p. 647.
23. Ibid., p. 673.

Fundamentals for the Future

TEN

The history of the United States has been the story of the steady rise of humanistic statism to power. Today, the control of civil government, public schools, and many churches has fallen into the hands of humanistic men who are fervent, even fanatical enemies of Christ and His Church. Homosexuals have come out of the closet to boast of and parade their life-style, whereas too many Christians have retreated into a hiding place to evade their responsibilities. While all this is true, it is not the whole story.

Napoleon defined history as "a lie agreed upon." American history will be such a lie if it leaves out the life and work of the Church, and especially what is happening now. As recently as 1955, in *The Twentieth Century Encyclopedia of Religious Knowledge*, edited by the Princeton Theological Seminary Church historian L. A. Loetscher, the entry for *Fundamentalism* reads: "See Biblicism; liberalism." The article on biblicism begins its brief survey with the medieval scholastics who held to "a strictly literal interpretation of the Bible." It refers to fundamentalism in two sentences only, one of them in opposition to it. The article on liberalism, three-and-a-half pages long, refers in passing to the opposition to humanism in the churches by fundamentalism, but says little more.

Even in 1955, fundamentalism was strong, and by 1975, between 50 and 55 million Americans over eighteen years of age described themselves as born-again Christians. What had happened?

Early in the century, as against humanism and Darwinism in the churches, Christians had begun to assert the fundamentals of the faith. Although the movement had its roots in the late years of the nine-

169

teenth century, it was near the end of the first decade of the twentieth century, in 1909, that two Christian laymen set aside money to issue some volumes setting forth the fundamentals of biblical faith. These publications were sent to three hundred thousand ministers, missionaries, and Christian workers all over the world. Their greatest impact was in the United States.

The articles were written by men from a variety of churches and theological backgrounds: Canon Dyson Hague of the Episcopal Church in Canada, Dr. F. Bettex of Germany, W. H. Griffith Thomas, James Orr, George L. Robertson, George Frederick Wright, M. G. Kyle, James M. Gray, A. T. Pierson, Arno C. Gaebelein, Thomas Whitelaw of Scotland, Robert E. Speer, B. B. Warfield, R. A. Torrey, Lord Lyttleton, Bishop H. C. G. Monk, John Timothy Stone, E. G. Trumbull, G. Campbell Morgan, Philip Mauro, C. R. Erdman, Mrs. Jesse Penn-Lewis, George F. Pentecost, C. T. Studd, and many others from Europe and North America. The main-line churches were heavily represented; Calvinism and Arminianism were on the battle line together.

From the institutional perspective, the years 1910-1940 were a disaster. One major church denomination after another broke with the biblical faith to favor modernism and humanism. The roll call of losses in those years is a dramatic one. The battle was most bitterly and intensely fought from 1920-1936 within the old Presbyterian Church USA, under the leadership of J. Gresham Machen. The battle was lost. From the perspective of the modernists, the battle was over. They controlled most denominations and seminaries and most church buildings, missionary agencies, and boards. The battle seemed to be over, with victory for the humanists.

This surface appearance was, however, deceptive. A leakage to new Bible-believing churches, or to those still holding to the faith, began to turn into a flood. In 1940 the Southern Baptists were mainly a *southern* church. The war helped move some members northward and westward but, even more, many turned to it as the Bible-believing church, and it became a national body. Bible-believing churches with a variety of polities began to proliferate, and the modernist churches began a steady decline in membership. Modernist congregations with a few thousand members on the books sometimes did well, by the late 1970s and early 1980s, to have two hundred in the pews. This had been especially true in the north and the west.

At the same time the number of new seminaries, Bible schools, Bible colleges, missionary boards, and Christian schools began to multiply. America's worldwide missionary work began to change hands: the modernist churches lost their missionary concern, and the Bible-believing churches, new and old, began to increase their missions with renewed effectiveness.

To understand the fundamentalism-modernist controversy, it is important to glance at the struggle within the old Presbyterian Church USA. In that church, the General Assembly in 1923 issued a deliverance which summed up the five essential doctrines of the faith common to all Christians—Protestant, Roman Catholic, and Greek Orthodox. In 1924 the modernists in that church answered with the Auburn Affirmation. The Deliverance of 1923 summed up the essence of the "fundamentals" which had been set forth earlier. The first doctrine of the deliverance affirmed the infallibility and inerrancy of Scripture; the Auburn Affirmation denied it. The second affirmed the virgin birth; Auburn declared that other opinions here and elsewhere "are worthy of all confidence and fellowship." The third doctrine of the deliverance declared that "Christ offered up Himself a sacrifice to satisfy divine justice and to reconcile us to God"; Auburn insisted on a vague statement and held the historic view of the blood atonement to be one theory among many. The fourth doctrine of the deliverance sets forth Christ's bodily resurrection from the dead, His ascension, and His intercessory power at the right hand of the Father; Auburn stated that the resurrection need not have been a bodily one. The fifth doctrine upheld the miracle-working power of Christ, while Auburn simply held that "in His earthly ministry He wrought many mighty works," refusing to hold that Christ's works were supernatural.[1]

The center of this battle soon shifted elsewhere, outside the Presbyterian Church. The General Assembly of that church had insisted that it "has all the power the Church would have if it were possible to convene the Church together in one place." It made itself the official interpreter of the church's constitution and the Bible, and all members were to abide by its decisions, whatever they might be. The church had replaced the Bible.[2] The fundamentalists were those who held that the Bible governs the Church.

For a time, the word *fundamentalism* was claimed for the separatist, Arminian, and dispensational churches. In recent years, a variety of politics and theologies have been covered by that term as these various churches have come together informally to take a common stand against humanism, statism, statist controls over the Church, and similar problems.

In the early 1970s an issue began to surface that was destined to accelerate bringing together the Christians of all denominations who believed in the sanctity of life. The right-to-life of the unborn child was being questioned by the humanist element in American society. *Roe vs. Wade*, the 1973 Supreme Court decision legalizing abortion, brought the issue into sharp focus. The Court held that unborn children are not persons protected by the United States Constitution.[3]

The dangers inherent in this judicial decision are strongly emphasized by Yale law professor John Hart Ely, who favors abortion. Ely's general opinion is that the *Roe vs. Wade* decision is "frightening." Writing in the *Yale Law Journal*, he states: "It is bad because it is bad constitutional law and gives almost no sense of an obligation to try to be."[4] The Supreme Court members allowed their own personal feelings, rather than the provisions of the Constitution, to determine the decision.

The *Roe vs. Wade* decision and the aftermath of abortion on demand, which resulted in the death of millions of unborn babies, gave rise to numerous right-to-life organizations which cut across all Christian, ethnic, and economic groups in America. Such organizations as Eagle Forum, Pro Family Forum, American Life Lobby, Catholics United for the Faith, Right to Life, and many others have mobilized to oppose abortion and the related issues.

The pro-family/pro-life movement embraces the belief in the sanctity of life, the worth of an individual, and the importance of traditional family life as the cornerstone of American society. The concerted efforts of these groups are creating an awareness on the part of the average citizen and bringing to bear much greater influence in the legislative and judicial processes at the state and national level. Politicians are beginning to realize the power of this great avalanche of concern.

By 1975 the diverse trends began to develop. First, state and federal bureaucracies became fearful of the growing power of the Christian-school movement. They saw it as a means whereby conservative evangelism was increasing its strength and reaching countless parents through their children. As a result, the persecution of Christian schools began. Ministers and parents were jailed in some states as they resisted these violations of the separation of Church and State.

Second, politicians suddenly became aware of the rapid growth of conservative evangelism and its potential political power. Jimmy Carter, an obscure candidate, gained national attention, the Democratic presidential nomination, and the election when he declared himself to be a born-again Christian. In 1980 Carter, Anderson, and Reagan all professed themselves to be born-again Christians. The politicians had suddenly recognized the political potential of biblical fundamentalism and were anxious to appease the fundamentalists with a superficial affirmation.

Two contradictory movements were thus under way: one, an attack on Christianity, the other, an attempt to mitigate this assault through confession. Both of these movements are testimonies to the dramatic change cascading forth in the United States; both witness to the great and growing faith in evidence on all sides.

At the same time, very great changes were in process with fundamentalism. Its earlier image was that of the "fighting fundy," of negation, separation, and hostility. ("Fundy," of course, was a derogatory shortening of "fundamentalist.") These tempers were legitimate and understandable, given the fact that so many men were driven out of local churches built with their labor and money, abused in church assemblies, and treated as fools or ignorant men. The "fighting fundy" has quietly given way to the man of positive action. This has meant the patient recapture of churches and seminaries, or the establishment of new ones. It has meant not antimodernist preaching as much as a sound program of biblical teaching to establish believers in the faith. It has meant a return to conservative evangelism. It has meant Christian schools, missions, colleges, ministries to the old and to the young, to criminals and delinquents, and other areas of Christian service. The modernists and liberals wage a paper war of negation. The center of Christian faith and action is now with conservative evangelism—the new fundamentalism of a positive Christian mission, life, and action.

Those who look to the troubled and unhappy past will, like Lot's wife, be forever condemned to it. Those who allow the present evils, which at times echo Sodom and Gomorrah, to overwhelm them are denying the power of God. The Lord who destroyed the world before the Flood, broke the power of Egypt, Assyria, Babylon, Rome, and other tyrannies, is the same today and forever. He is raising up men to be more than conquerors in Him (Romans 8:37). The future will be commanded by those who in Christ work for it patiently, with grace, hope, and love, and who even now are establishing the churches, Christian schools, and institutions, to remake the world in Christ. It is a future being realized in Christ's people entering into medicine, law, business, the work force, politics, and in every calling, to serve the Lord Jesus Christ.

The twentieth century has witnessed two great missionary forces at work. The first is world communism. Its death toll is easily 100 million or more. It has been an evil, destructive force, now at its height, with serious and fatal seeds of decay at its center.

The other great missionary force has been the Christian renaissance, born out of the fundamentalist-modernist controversy. It is now at work changing lives, creating institutions, and striving to make all things new in Christ. The power of the faith is manifest in every continent; it transforms its enemies.

When Adoniram Judson saw his missionary work in Burma destroyed, his presses smashed, his converts killed or scattered, and he himself in a filthy dungeon, his captors taunted him, asking, "What are your prospects now?"

Judson answered, "As bright as the promises of God!"

Can we have any less faith? Our prospects are marked by the many assured and reliable promises of God.

Chapter 10 Notes

1. Edwin H. Rian, *The Presbyterian Conflict* (Grand Rapids: Eerdmans, 1940), pp. 29–59.
2. Ibid., p. 207.
3. John W. Whitehead, *The Stealing of America* (Westchester, Illinois: Crossway Books, 1983), pp. 48–49.
4. John W. Whitehead, *The Second American Revolution* (Elgin, Illinois: David C. Cook Publishing Co., 1982), p. 124.